THIS IS FOR
EVERYONE

As leader of Congregation Bene Shalom/HAD in Skokie, Illinois, **RABBI DOUGLAS GOLDHAMER** is the only full-time rabbi serving a deaf Jewish community in the United States. He received his rabbinic ordination, MHL, and Doctor of Divinity from Hebrew Union College, Cincinnati, and currently serves as President of Hebrew Seminary of the Deaf, where he is Professor of Jewish Mysticism. Goldhamer is also a nationally known artist.

MELINDA STENGEL is a psychotherapist in private practice in Evanston, Illinois. A graduate of the University of Wisconsin with a degree in special education, she has a Master's Degree in Social Work from the University of Chicago. Melinda presents at many professional conferences and is the parent counselor in the early intervention program for deaf babies and their families at Northwestern University.

The Healer, by Rabbi Douglas Goldhamer, 1998, 23" × 30", mixed media on paper.

This is for Everyone

*Universal Principles of Healing Prayer
and the Jewish Mystics*

RABBI DOUGLAS GOLDHAMER, DD

MELINDA STENGEL, LCSW

Published for
the Paul Brunton Philosophic Foundation by
LARSON PUBLICATIONS

COVER ART: Detail from *The Healer,* 1998, by
Rabbi Douglas Goldhamer

International Standard Book Number: 0-943914-93-0
Library of Congress Catalog Card Number: 99-73535

Published for the Paul Brunton Philosophic Foundation by
Larson Publications
4936 NYS Route 414
Burdett, New York 14818 USA

06 05 04 03 02 01 00
10 9 8 7 6 5 4 3 2

THIS BOOK IS DEDICATED

to the memory of my teacher Rabbi Dan Dresher
and to my wife and best friend
Peggy Bagley

They inspire me to study,
They inspire me to write,
They inspire me to paint,
They inspire me to reach God.

—D.G.

To my husband Jim, my children,
Jameson and Katie Rose,
my mother, Mary Arant, and
my sister, Mary Anne Delacenserie,
for their belief in me.

—M.S.

CONTENTS

5: **Healing Prayer**

6: **The Commandment to Rejoice**

7: **Let Us Make Man in Our Image**

8: **Alternative Meditations**

9: **Our Prayer Group**

ACKNOWLEDGMENTS

I WANT to take this opportunity to thank my synagogue Congregation Bene Shalom/Hebrew Association of the Deaf. Our community has been very patient with me this past year as I have worked on this book, even though it sometimes interfered with my time with the congregation. Frequently, I had to rearrange individual appointments with people, and yet the members of my community continually encouraged me to write this book. I especially want to thank Nona Balk, our temple president, and our wonderful board, whose members always had a cheerful word of support for me. When I couldn't see students, two of my rabbinical students from the Hebrew Seminary of the Deaf, Mark Cohen and Steve Katz, generously taught my pupils. And Yvette Freedberg has always been there for me in all emergencies.

I want to thank my wife, Peggy Bagley, who corrected my spelling and grammar and offered excellent insights and ideas that were indispensable to me. I can honestly say there would be no book without Peggy. She worked as hard on the manuscript as I did.

I also want to extend a special thanks to Melinda for being my writing partner and for working with me on our special healing projects. Our healing group, which meets every other Wednesday, is a great group of people with enormous faith in God. I am always inspired that Christians and Jews can come together and worship and embrace the one God with joy and faith.

I also want to thank my most patient editor, Paul Cash, whose continuous advice and support will always be remembered.

Praised are You, O Lord our God, the Spirit within us, who supports us, keeps us alive, and allows us to accomplish anything we do.

RABBI DOUGLAS GOLDHAMER

I ALSO would like to thank Congregation Bene Shalom for the support, warmth, and generosity that have made the Healing Prayer classes and the writing of this book wonderful experiences. A special thanks goes to Rabbi Douglas Goldhamer. Words cannot express my gratitude. He has been as kind to me as anyone I have ever known.

I would also like to thank my husband, Jim, who was a continuous source of encouragement and help, and Peggy Bagley who was always there with warmth, humor, and a variety of remarkable skills.

With the Healing Prayer group, I have experienced again that, when one gives, one gets back tenfold. Each member has become a special person in my life.

Our editor, Paul Cash, guided and encouraged us each step of the way. My thanks to him for offering us this remarkable opportunity.

To my family—Jameson, Katie Rose, Mom, Mary Anne, John, Tony, Phil, Tom, Steve, Mike, and Uncle Bill Arant—thanks for the enthusiasm and love.

This book is only the "icing on the cake" for all that I have been given by all of these wonderful people and by learning to experience God.

MELINDA STENGEL

PREFACE

MELINDA   During a profoundly dark, painful period of my life, when
one of my children had been very sick for a long time, I
did something I would never have normally done. I asked a rabbi if
he ever met with, taught, prayed with, or guided someone who was
not only not a member of his congregation, but not even Jewish.

He looked puzzled for a moment and then replied, "Melinda, this
is for *everyone*."

"For *everyone*?" I asked.

"Of course. There are universal principles that transcend all religions and there are special prayers for physical healing that have worked
for many people. I can teach you." He definitely had my attention.

"Oh, but I have a really bad attitude about God and spirituality. I
just can't put belief in an all-loving God together with all of the terrible suffering in the world."

"I believe that God does not want for you to suffer," the Rabbi
said. "And, there are ways to learn to have faith plus special prayers
and meditations to ask for what you need and want. I will teach you."

I almost yelled, "You mean it's okay to ask God? I am not spoiled
or selfish or too attached or controlling, or any of the things I have
been told my whole life!?!"

"It is okay to ask. In fact, God wants you to ask," was the wonderful reply. Those were the most liberating words I had ever heard.
Maybe I could believe in this kind of God. And I could actually *do*
things to increase my faith!

During some of the darkest, worst days of my life, he said to me,
"Melinda, this works." And, it does. It works for Rabbi Douglas, who

has dedicated his life to this study and practice. And it works for me—who began with a truckload of doubt and a bad attitude. And it has worked for many others, some of whom share their stories in the pages that follow.

This is a book about actually experiencing God through healing and learning faith. You will learn universal principles that are part of, yet transcend all religions. You will learn specific ways to experience God and effect healing through eliminating the "space" between you and God.

RABBI   In 1972, I was ordained as a rabbi by Hebrew Union
DOUGLAS   College in Cincinnati. I was ordained not only because I passed all the academic requirements that are necessary to be a rabbi, but also because I showed the seminary that I was committed to Torah and to the Jewish people. I still am committed to Torah and to the Jewish people, in my own community and around the world. This is my life. But, if it is possible to have a greater commitment, it is my commitment to God and to all people, regardless of their religion. I believe that if someone accepts that there is a Divine Force, and if she or he becomes one with this Power, then more than ordinary things can happen. Melinda and I have tried to illustrate this in our book.

The reason I have used many Jewish meditative practices is because I am familiar with these meditations. I use them in my daily life and in the lives of the people who visit me regularly. These meditations work with Catholics and Quakers and Jews and others. They are for all people. I am also confident that other meditative practices of other religions are equally good. The principle of this text is to teach that everyone who understands and practices the unity of God and makes the unity of God an integral part of their life can, together with their physicians, effect spiritual and physical healings that they never thought possible.

The most important thing Rabbi Dresher, my teacher, taught me was to pray with *kavvanah*—as I explain in chapter one. Our tradition also teaches not to make our prayer a "fixed" prayer. Rabbi Dresher encouraged me to pray differently each day. I remember he often said, "Even the same prayer has to be different every day. When the same is different, it is no longer the same."

This book is filled with meditations. Learn them. Practice them. Do them. But don't do them as I do them. Do them as *you* do them. Make them your own. And as you make these prayers and meditative exercises your own, you will become closer and closer to God—until you and God become one. Then, with faith and with the Greater Mind, there is no limit to your prayers.

Rabbi Dresher also taught me something even more important than faith and meditative exercises. He taught me the importance of being a good person. Being a good person does not only mean saying the right things and speaking the right prayers. Being a good person means doing good things on a regular basis.

This means sharing your money regularly, every week, with people who need money. This means sharing your time regularly every week with people who need your time. This means sharing your knowledge regularly every week with people who would benefit from your knowledge. This means becoming like God.

In the many years that I have prayed with many people, I have seen that it is not enough to do the right meditations in the right way with the right *kavvanah*. It's not enough to pray with faith and with joy and in the Greater Mind. People who pray and who want God to reside within them *should* do these things and should practice regularly. But they should *also* practice the Presence of God every day. This means we should try to be kind and compassionate to those we love and even to those we don't love every day. In this way, our souls become fertile ground for the Spirit of God. And when we do our meditative exercises, their efficacy will indeed be greater.

• • •

Each chapter is organized into three parts. The first part is written by Rabbi Douglas Goldhamer, and teaches a Universal Principle. The second part is written by Melinda Stengel, and explains a Liberating

Concept. The third part is a "How To" section written by Rabbi Douglas; it explains, in simple steps, one or more practical techniques you can use to activate God's energies within you.

All Christian Bible references are from The Holy Bible, New Revised Standard Version, unless noted otherwise. Hebrew Biblical references are from the Holy Scriptures, published by the Jewish Publication Society of America in 1982.

The "Notes" section at the back of the book contains useful comments that could not easily be worked into the text. The "Sources" section contains source references on quotations, etc. Translations of Hebrew texts have been done by Rabbi Douglas unless otherwise noted.

1: GOD IS A FORCE IN THE UNIVERSE AND IN US

Universal Principle: God is within us

RABBI DOUGLAS   I WAS RAISED and educated in Montreal as an Orthodox Jewish person. I was taught that God is reached through *mitzvot*, which means through commandments (good works) and through prayer. I have since learned that good works and faith are not enough to reach God, to unite one with God. They are important stepping stones that put us in an environment to reach God. But beyond good works and faith, there is one step that we have to take in order to connect with God. The purpose of this book is to teach that one extra step.

We must first know that God is in the universe, a natural force of love and intelligence. Then we must learn specific ways to bring God within us, to activate God within us. To know God, we must experience God.

I learned this through a remarkable series of events that took place twenty-four years ago after I was diagnosed with a painful, potentially fatal illness. These events led me to a new understanding of God and prayer.

One winter day, twenty-four years ago, I had severe pain in my leg. Saying, "You needed to go yesterday," my doctor sent me immediately to the hospital. At that time my only companion was Ritchie, my dog, and he was unable to help me pack, so I packed alone. That day, I entered the hospital.

The doctors tried to eliminate the blood clot in my leg through medicine, but that didn't work. I had surgery for it and was in the hospital for a long time. The recuperation was very slow. I walked with a cane for years because the pain was so severe. The pain and the circulatory problems increased and, after a second surgery, the recovery was even slower. It was extremely frightening and frustrating.

My brother, who is a psychiatrist, suggested consulting medical texts. I was a student at the University of Chicago at the time, and in that library I discovered that the syndrome I had is called Klippel-Trenaunay. This syndrome is called an "orphan disease" because it is so rare. There were only twenty-two cases reported during that year. Money is not spent on research for that reason. To my horror, the sources at the University of Chicago Library also revealed that the worst treatment for this disease was surgery!

My condition continued to worsen so Peggy, my wife, and I went to Northwestern University Hospital in 1982. The head of vascular surgery said that my left leg would have to be amputated soon because gangrene would set in within the year, and my right leg might also need to be amputated. I was devastated and frightened. I prayed the traditional way, the way I had been taught to pray, but it seemed that either God said no or there was no efficacy to my prayer.

I could not accept God saying no, so I continued to pray. One night I was watching Christian television. Now you might think it odd for a rabbi to watch Christian television, but I watched because the ministers were inspirational teachers in the art of giving sermons.

I learned this from my mother. She was fascinated with preachers of all religions. Even though she was Orthodox, she was a universalist and regularly taught me that God is the same God for all people.

When I went to Hebrew Union College to study for the rabbinate, for example, my mother handed me an old shoe box. I was puzzled by the gift until I found within the box scores and scores of old sermons written by Bishop Fulton Sheen, Reverend Norman Vincent Peale, and Rabbi Harry Joshua Stern. So, I was brought up with a reverence for preachers and preaching. And it wasn't odd, after all, for me, a rabbi, to watch preachers on Christian television.

This particular night, however, there was a preacher who was talking about healing prayer. This was a new and fascinating concept for me. So I called him and explained my need. I told this minister that he seemed like a fine man—indeed, he inspired me. But I also told him that I just was not comfortable with praying to Jesus, because Jesus was not part of my tradition. I asked if he happened to know a rabbi or a Jewish educator who had similar thoughts on healing prayer. Amazingly, this Christian preacher knew of a Hasidic rabbi in Rogers Park, not far from me.

KAVVANAH

I subsequently met with Rabbi Daniel Dresher privately and regularly for almost seven months until I was cured. To some extent, we prayed the traditional Jewish prayers—many of the words were the same as in the *Siddur* (Jewish Prayer Book). To my great delight, Rabbi Dresher opened my eyes to a new kind of prayer—added a crucial internal dynamic to the prayer. He taught me *kavvanah*.

Kavvanah is a Hebrew term. It means to do something with a mind that is totally focused, not perfunctory, not with the mind wandering, not just saying the words, but with focused attention and intention. To pray with *kavvanah* means to pray with the intention completely focused and to pray from the heart or soul. I found praying with *kavvanah* to be profoundly inspiring.

After seven months of praying with *kavvanah*, I did not need the cane again. I was completely cured—much to my doctors' astonishment and my joy.

I have learned more since that time through studying and praying with and for people and seeing the healing results. One of the most influential books I read during my early learning was written by a Christian healer named Agnes Sanford. Remarkably, Mrs. Sanford's teaching is in many ways the same as Rabbi Dresher's. She emphasized the same crucial elements and enhanced my learning and skill, becoming a spiritual guide to me through her many books. Here was a devout Christian speaking the same words as a devout Orthodox Jew. They came from totally different cultures, and both of them convinced me that the principles of prayer and healing are universal—that is, they are included in all religions, yet transcend all religions.

When Melinda first came to me seeking spirituality, faith, and healing, we began to discuss the universal principles that transcend any particular religion. We saw that Catholicism has one set of rituals, practices, and ethics. Judaism has its own set of rituals, practices, and ethics. Each belief system and religious community—including Buddhists, Protestants, Muslims, Quakers, and all the others—has its own practices.

Each of us was taught a different concept of God. Melinda was taught that God is reached through atonement, penance, goodness, suffering, and through Jesus. I was taught that God is reached through prayer and good works. We also saw that there are principles that transcend our individual communities.

So, in my studying and learning with Rabbi Dresher, I added the internal dynamic of *kavvanah* to my prayers for healing and was completely cured in seven months. Jewish scholarship maintains that the word *kavvanah* may mean intention, concentration, devotion, purpose, right spirit, pondering, meditation, mystery. The word *kavvanah* connotes all these things. Praying with *kavvanah* eliminates the space between us and God. God is activated within us. We ignite or inspire the Divine Force to come together with us, and this effects physical healing.

What I have experienced is that there is a God—but this God is unlike anything human. If we say God is good, or smart, or gentle, that He or She sees, we do this because we use our normal, intellectual, cognitive tendency to give human attributes to God. In my work through the last fifteen years, I have seen that God is not like this at all. From my experience, *God is like a force, an ineffable force, that cannot be explained intellectually and must be experienced to begin to be known.*

If we can begin to pray to the God within us, instead of looking to God who lives in the heavens, we can begin to eliminate the illness within us. So our task is to discover the God that exists *in this universe* and bring this Presence within us. Praying with *kavvanah* is the extra, all-important step—beyond faith and good works—to activate God within you.

Then, when we know God is within us, we can learn to bring the spark of God within us, out of us. Then the God within and the God without become One, as we and God become One. This is what is meant by the special Hebrew prayer, *Shema:* "Hear O Israel, the Lord our God, the Lord is One." This prayer is a key prayer in the Jewish faith. It affirms the existence of one God and that this one God must be worshipped regularly. The Jewish people have the duty of reciting this prayer regularly two times every day, in their regular prayer quorum (*minyan*). In addition, many Jews recite this prayer upon retiring every night. It is also the prayer that should be on the lips of every Jew at death.

This prayer also finds its way into the Christian tradition. In the Gospel according to Mark, Mark goes to Jesus and asks him what is the most important prayer. Jesus answers, "Hear O Israel, the Lord our God, the Lord is One." (Mark 12:29)

Judaism teaches that it is not enough to just recite the prayer. We have to recite the prayers with the proper *kavvanah*. It is a Jewish tradition that when we pray the *Shema*, we cup our hands with our eyes closed, so that we visualize the Divine Light of God while reciting this prayer. This is called *kavvanah*.

It is a general principle of Judaism that the fulfillment of religious duties requires *kavvanah*. This means that when we perform a religious duty, such as saying the blessing before the meal, or praying the *Shema*, or kissing the *mezuzah*[1] on entering a home, we must do this religious duty with all our heart. That is, when we do this religious duty, we must not be thinking of something else. So, when you kiss the *mezuzah*, for example, or say the blessing before the meal, or recite the *Shema*, your mind must be focused on the words that you utter and your heart must be involved in what you are doing. You must do this *mitzvah* with all your heart. This is what the rabbis mean when they say that the fulfillment of religious duties requires *kavvanah:* Duties must be fulfilled with intention (not just going through the motions) and devout concentration.

SHEKHINA

The Hebrew Kabbalah uses mystical meditations—visual meditations and auditory *mantras*—that are called *kavvanot*. These spiritual exercises cause us to focus with concentration and intention on the Presence of God. You can use these mystical meditations—some of which are included in this book—to bring God into you. God is like a well of marvelous energy that we must learn to tap to bring within us.

The major textbook of Jewish law, the *Shulkhan Aruch*, written in sixteenth-century Palestine by Joseph Caro, also uses the Hebrew term *kavvan* to indicate true prayer. In *Orach Chayyim* in "The Laws of Prayer," the *Shulkhan Aruch* maintains that when you pray, you must pray as if the Presence of God is before you, ridding you of all foreign and troubling thoughts, until your only thought is that you are before a great king, who is the Ruler of the Universe. The *Shulkhan Aruch* goes on to say that this method of *kavvanah* involves prayer with all your heart. *Kavvanah* means to empty one's heart of every other care and regard oneself as standing before the Presence of God. This is the true method of pious people who spiritually isolate themselves and meditate.

I used these methods of Jewish prayer and studied other religions, including the famous Ibn al-Arabi of Islam, and I saw that these approaches are universal principles, shared by all faiths. Ibn 'Arabi (1165–1240), the great Sufi mystic, wrote in his book *Journey to the Lord of Power,* "If you want to enter the Presence of the Truth and receive from Him without intermediary and you desire intimacy with Him, this will not be appropriate as long as your heart acknowledges any lordship other than His."

The first universal principle I learned when I prayed with *kavvanah* is that the traditional idea that God and Man/Woman are separate does not promote healing. As said earlier, we have to discover that God is in the universe first and then bring that God within us so that we can become one. We have to bring Her within us. I say "Her" because we have to think of God as the feminine power within us. This feminine aspect of God is the *Shekhina*. God has many manifestations, and the Kabbalists believe that the manifestation that is most immanent to us is God in Her feminine aspect. This is the immanent Presence in our world. We have to learn to *Practice the Presence of God*, to practice the *Shekhina* of God.

In our Sabbath evening and morning services, some of our prayers refer to God as "She." Occasionally, a member of our synagogue will ask me if I am only introducing "she" to achieve a politically correct situation. Jewish theology in the early part of the First Millenium used the feminine nature of God, the *Shekhina*, to explain the immanent nature of Her being. It was the *Shekhina* who accompanied the Jews in exile, and it was She who manifested Herself in the ancient Temple. Yet, it was the male aspect of God who transcendentally stood on Mt. Sinai, bellowing out the first two commandments in a voice so loud and strong that Moses himself had to read the next eight, because the people became frightened. This transcendent male deity is called *Hakadosh Barukh Hu*, the Holy One, Blessed be He. When the Messiah comes, the Jews believe that the feminine aspect of God and the male aspect of God will merge and "the Lord shall be One."

The *Shulkhan Aruch* maintains that when we pray, we must feel and think as if the *Shekhina* is before us.

We see a similar concept in Talmud, Shabbat 22b, which teaches us that the light from the menorah testifies to the *Shekhina* residing in the world. It is also teaching that the *Shekhina* is always near, and it is for us to focus on Her and to invite Her into our lives. Also, Proverbs 20:27, like the Talmud, identifies God and light.

We must actually *experience* God in us. We and God are One; everything in the universe is One. There is no separation.

LIGHT

The term "Light" is favored by the mystics—Jewish and non-Jewish—to describe the various manifestations and emanations of the Divinity. Rabbi Joseph Albo in his text, *Sefer Ikkarim*, identifies light and God because

1. The existence of light cannot be denied.
2. Light is not a corporeal thing.
3. Light delights the soul.

The Jewish Kabbalist Joseph Ergas in his famous book *Shomer Emunim,* also identifies light with God because

1. Light spreads itself instantaneously.

2. Light *per se* never changes.

3. Light is essential to life in general.

Light illumines all physical objects and can penetrate all transparent objects. In the Christian tradition, the Scriptures identify Jesus with the Light. "I am the Light." (John 8:12)

The magnum opus of Kabbalistic literature, the *Zohar,* in part I (50b–51a), uses a candle as an image for divine unity. This Zoharic passage is related to Proverbs 20:27, "The Light (candle) of the Lord is my soul."

Rabbi Dresher referred me to all these sources, encouraging me to understand that if we want to be "heard" by the Light of the World, we must, as the *Shulkhan Aruch* states, stand before God's Presence, and we must also invite God within us. We must take this Biblical proverb and we must use this text to eliminate the space between us and God.

As a practicing rabbi, I often ask my Sunday School children where they think God is. Some claim God is in the heavens, others maintain that God is everywhere—north, south, east, west, up, down. Still others maintain that God is within us.

When I was a boy—even when I was a young rabbi before I met the Hasidic rabbi, Rabbi Dresher—I used to imagine God as a compassionate being who, when addressed, would respond in a compassionate way. I always imagined what Cecil B. DeMille showed me in the movie, *The Ten Commandments:* When Moses went up the mountain and spoke to God, God spoke to him and gave him the Torah. Our Judeo-Christian-Islamic tradition teaches this, that God handed the sacred law to Moses. When we image that picture, we visualize the Deity. We visualize Moses and we see the Deity giving Moses the Torah. This picture contains three representations—God, Moses, and Torah. There is God and there is Moses, and there is a space between God and Moses—albeit this space is filled with the Torah.

Using these sources, I discovered this universal principle that is included in, yet transcends, all religions: *If we can eliminate the space that exists between us and God, if we can become one with God, then we can alleviate illness in our lives.* This is not done in place of traditional medicine, but is done working with our physicians and other physical healers.

How can we bring God within us? How is this possible? One way we can do this is by a meditation found in the *Zohar.* This meditation is called "The Candle Meditation." The "How To" section of this chapter will explain how you can do this meditation.

Liberating Concept: Asking God

God does not want us to suffer; we can ask God for anything

MELINDA   This is a story of how a Catholic-raised gal came to be teaching and writing with a rabbi and about her experiences with healing meditation and prayer.

I never would have dreamed that I would be doing this. I am a fairly traditional psychotherapist and, until now, have always been a private person. The change came when the prayer and meditations worked for me in such a spectacular way. I told Rabbi Douglas that he should find a way to share this with more people, and he asked me to teach and write with him. Basically I am here because the prayer and meditations this book teaches worked for me.

My journey to spirituality began with a 1950s Catholic upbringing. On the positive side, Catholicism gave me the desire to be a good person and to help others. But, even as a child, I could never put the belief in an all-loving God together with the terrible suffering in the world. Suffering was the result of sin, we were taught—if not my personal sin, then the Original Sin of Adam and Eve. Suffering was necessary in order to get to heaven and, therefore, part of God's plan.

Since that time, Catholicism has changed enormously. Now my children in school are learning, among other things, to have a positive relationship with God—one based on connecting with God and becoming better people.

When my son graduated from eighth grade, the priest at High

Mass began by welcoming people of all faiths. He emphasized that whatever name we give to God, we all belong to one family.

A number of years ago, when I was a beginning therapist, a client had a terrifying psychosis. Sitting with this woman's suffering, I had to conclude that no one could have done something bad enough to deserve this—and what kind of God would so terribly punish this poor woman because of someone else's sin!?! It didn't make sense. Even if heaven were magnificent, it could never be worth the suffering right there in front of me.

About the same time, I read Dostoyevsky's *The Brothers Karamazov*. In that book, one of the brothers, Ivan, ponders the nature of God and heaven. He thinks that heaven can't be worth the price of the tears of one abused child. The suffering of just that one child is enough for him to say that he was most respectfully returning the ticket of ad-mission to heaven. As Ivan said: "But then there are the children, and what am I to do with them? That is the question I can-not answer. . . . It is entirely incomprehensible why they, too, should have to suffer and why they should have to buy harmony (of heaven) by their sufferings."

That question was unanswerable for me, too, but my mind would not let it go. What does the suffering of children or the mentally ill have to do with heaven? Unsatisfactory answers to these questions left me with a bad attitude and a spiritual hole for the next fourteen years. It was not that I gave up the search, but I didn't know where to look. I deeply wanted spirituality but did not have a clue how to get it.

And then, about four years ago, after I had worked many years with people who were suffering, one of my children got very sick and I experienced terrible suffering first-hand. The worst pain in the world comes when something bad happens to one of your children. Words can hardly express that pain, but the words that always come to mind were spoken by a parent of a young deaf child who had had menin-gitis and could no longer walk. This Dad described the feelings as anguish and despair. Yes, those were the true words.

After two years of extensive searching, we finally found the right treatment for my child's constant headaches. My own depression and anxiety, however, stuck with me.

It was an excruciating time, but this painful crisis propelled me to do a life-changing thing: to see Rabbi Douglas three years ago.

I had known Rabbi Douglas professionally for fifteen years. My work as a psychotherapist in private practice and as a parent-counselor at Northwestern University has included many deaf people, and Rabbi Douglas' congregation was founded for deaf people and their families. Clients and friends often talked about this man's everyday small and large kindnesses. People would say: "I talked to the Rabbi and he did this," or "I talked to the Rabbi and he said that," or "I talked to the Rabbi and he helped me with this," or "The Rabbi called me yesterday to see how I was doing," and on and on and on.

Henry James once said: "Three things in human life are important. The first is to be kind. The second is to be kind, and the third is to be kind." That described this rabbi. Rabbi Douglas is the kind of person so many of us wish we could be.

I occasionally went to services and marveled at his faith and joy. His faith in God both amazed me and, to be very frank, made me quite jealous. I would say to myself: "That man's got something I want." But I didn't have a clue how to get it. Well, eventually I found out how to get it, and that's why I'm in on this book with Rabbi Douglas.

One thing that misery can do is make people do things and take chances they *never* would take under ordinary circumstances. I asked Rabbi Douglas if he ever taught, gave guidance to, or prayed with someone who was not only not a member of his congregation, but not even Jewish.

His answer astonished me.

I remember that he looked really puzzled for a moment and then said, "Melinda, this is for everyone." As if—wasn't that obvious?

Well, actually, no. It wasn't obvious, given my childhood religious education. And it probably wouldn't be to most people, given the religious education most of today's adults got as children. Like most religions of the day, the Catholicism of the 1950s was built on the "us and them" philosophy. The "us'es" (we) were going to heaven and the "thems" (they) were going to hell. Because of childhood experiences and my values, I couldn't buy in: I could never have a belief system or spirituality that was based on excluding anyone.

So, no, it was not obvious to me. But I could believe in the kind of God Rabbi Douglas seemed to know. He taught me several universal principles that are both part of all religions and transcend each one of them. This concept gave me a new way to spirituality: This is for everyone.

I went into Rabbi Douglas's office every week with my doubts, especially about a God who required suffering in order to get into heaven and avoid eternal damnation. If that were God's plan, it just didn't seem fair. Had any of us asked to be in this situation, with our poor, inadequate human brains and psyches in the first place? Samuel Butler said, "Life is like playing a violin in public and learning the instrument as one goes on." A perfect description.

When I was growing up, my relationship with God was based on the fear of going to hell. This was a "punishing Father" God who noted my tiniest sins. It was a great motivator to behave myself, but it did nothing for me spiritually. Albert Einstein spent his life pondering the physical and spiritual universe and concluded that he could not imagine a God who was but a reflection of our human frailty.

We tend to conceptualize a God modeled on our parents because that's how our minds work. We take information and fit it into what we already "know." From the time of birth, our minds are constantly trying to understand the world. In the book, *The Interpersonal World of the Human Infant,* researcher and psychiatrist Daniel Stern shows that from birth on, the human brain has a central tendency to form and test hypotheses about what is occurring in the world. Even infants have sophisticated cognitive abilities to process and understand information, including the ability to abstract, average, and represent information preverbally.

The very way that the human mind works makes it inevitable that we are constantly searching for meaning. We're neurologically programmed to work to understand, and we're always building on what was learned before. Children think about God as "parent-like" because they already have the model of "parent" in their minds. And, since children are psychologically egocentric, they believe that they are the cause of everything and are responsible for everything that happens. It is no wonder that we carry guilt for events and feelings from our young childhood and expect punishment from somewhere.

Einstein also said: "Strange is our situation here upon earth." I agree with him one hundred percent. We're all just trying to make sense of this crazy life. Each religion grapples with these issues and tries to make sense of what happens to each of us every day.

So, when Rabbi Douglas and I talked about suffering, and he said that he believes that God does not want us to suffer, and that suffering is not part of God's plan—these were some of the most liberating words I had ever heard. It was the first truly Liberating Concept I learned from Rabbi Douglas.

Moving beyond thinking of God as a punishing father, I could envision God as both female and male. During the Healing Prayer, I connect with the deep "feminine" aspect of God and myself—the love I experienced when cradling my babies. At other times, it feels right to refer to God as "He" and "Lord." These concepts simply express qualities that are in all of us regardless of gender.

This book presents a way to move beyond thinking of God as a punishing or rewarding parent or as strictly masculine or feminine. From my personal experience, this move takes nothing more than the ability to approach this with a "beginner's mind," to allow yourself to think about the universe in a different way and then to observe if this new way works for you. That is the only "proof" of any kind of belief.

I had no faith when I walked into Rabbi Douglas's office. One of the most remarkable things that Rabbi Douglas taught me is that a person can learn to have faith! That is the Liberating Concept that will be discussed in chapter two.

How to Do It

How to bring God inside; How to activate the God within

CANDLE MEDITATION

RABBI   How can we bring God within us? How is this possible?
DOUGLAS   We do this in many ways. One way is to do so by this
meditation found in the *Zohar*.2

When I do this meditation, I can experience God's Light within me any time of the day. Don't worry if this doesn't happen right away. It took me a while before I could learn to experience the Light simply by attending to it. It is important to practice, practice, practice.

Put a candle in a candle holder, light it, and face the candle. The candle represents the Light of God. God is Light in many religious traditions.

So, now there is the candle and there is you. And as there is a space between the candle and your body, so there is a "space" between God's Light and you. And if you want to practice the presence of God, you have to eliminate the space—you want to be one with God. So in this meditation, you invite the candle to come within you. Visualize the candle coming closer and closer toward you. Keep your eyes closed when you do this, so you can better visualize the movement of the candle.

As you visualize the candle coming toward you, recite Proverbs 20:27. "The Light of the Lord is my Soul." Recite this proverb as a *mantra*, an intensely focused sacred expression. Your mind is focused only on the candle coming inside you. You are using *kavvanah*.

As you repeat the *mantra* again and again, notice that the separation between you and the candle diminishes. The candle is the Light of God. You want to eliminate the separation between you and God. Bring the image of the candle within you and say the *mantra* until you are filled up with the Light of God. Until you and God are One.

Throughout the day, whether it be at the water cooler or taking a break from your reading assignment, or during your lunch hour, whatever you may be doing, imagine yourself filled with the Light of God. This will give you a connectedness to God that will inspire you all day.

If you would like to say the *mantra* in Hebrew, the Hebrew words are, "*Ner Adonai Nishmat Adam.*"

2: LEARNING FAITH

Universal Principle: Do it and faith will follow

RABBI DOUGLAS   I REMEMBER very clearly an incident that happened to me just after my bar mitzvah. It was an experience that occurred during one of my many surgeries as a child.

One of the symptoms of Klippel-Trenaunay Syndrome (at that time I didn't know I had this disease), is the uneven growth of different body limbs. My left leg had grown noticeably larger than my right leg and, when I turned fourteen, the doctors wanted to arrest the growth of the left leg so the right leg would catch up. I had the surgery.

My brother visited me in the hospital. Like any good brother, he brought me my favorite food—two hot dogs with lots of relish and mustard and golden brown french fries with salt and vinegar. I had gulped down the first hot dog and eaten some of the fries, and I was beginning to devour my second hot dog when two Orthodox rabbis entered my hospital room.

The men wore black hats, black pants, and long black coats, and each of them had a long black beard. I was terrified. The hot dogs weren't kosher. I was caught. I would surely go to hell. I don't know if the rabbis knew from the smell of the meat that the hot dogs weren't kosher. They didn't comment on my food, but they did say to me that my suffering and my pain were necessary—both to improve my character and to bring me closer to God. I remember them also telling me that I merited this condition in which I found myself.

When they left, I was devastated. This did not heighten my faith. On the contrary, it alienated me from the rigors of the Orthodox

Judaism that I was being brought up with. Even though I was being brought up in an Orthodox home, I did not keep kosher outside the home. As a child, I went to Orthodox *shul* (temple) every Saturday morning. After I finished Orthodox Jewish Grammar School, I studied Talmud regularly every week with a learned Talmud scholar, Mr. Lepkofsky. My mother kept two sets of dishes—one for dairy, one for meat. Our meat came from a kosher butcher shop.

On the High Holy Days, my mother stayed home and cooked and my father took his two sons to the Orthodox neighborhood *shul* to pray—where men and women sat separately. We boys used to stand up during the service, look over at the neighboring aisle, and try to catch a glimpse of a pretty girl's legs. I received my first personal prayer book and prayer shawl on my bar mitzvah. My Hebrew prayer book taught me that we must pray in Hebrew and that we, the Jewish people, were chosen for a sacred mission.

Interestingly, these experiences and the experience with the two rabbis in the hospital did not inspire faith in me. It was my mother who taught me faith. Granted, she used to sprinkle me with Lourdes water! And her favorite radio personality was Pastor Johnson, who loved to preach on the parables of Jesus Christ. Even though my mother did not embrace the divinity of Jesus, she saw in him a spark of the divine—the same spark she saw in Buddha, Confucius, Moses, and other great religious leaders.

So, from an early age I was torn between the rigors of Orthodoxy that my community practiced, and a universalism that my mother would teach me and show me at every opportunity she got. I chose the latter to be my guiding principle of faith. I felt that God was everywhere, and could be embraced equally by the Orthodox Rabbi Miller who lived next door to us and the Catholic dentist Dr. Georges Perrault who lived upstairs from us.

God for me was found in the Torah and also in the Koran and in Christian Scripture. I always knew that the greatest democrat was not Thomas Jefferson, but God. And from an early age, I knew I would follow Him anywhere. When the two rabbis told me that my leg pain was an instrument of God's teaching, I felt devastated.

Nonetheless, I did not abandon my faith in God.

What I had seen from an early age with regard to faith was corroborated by what Rabbi Dresher taught me, and what our Jewish religion teaches us.

Our Jewish religion teaches that after the ancient Israelites were given the sacred Torah, they exclaimed, "*Na'aseh ve-Neshma.* We will do it, then we will understand it." I remember learning this as a boy and realizing how this Biblical axiom conflicted with the secular axiom that I was taught in school. Our fourth, fifth, and sixth grade work books were called *Think and Do.* This was the opposite of what my religious principles taught us—to do and think.

When I went to Rabbi Dresher and asked him to help me and teach me how to pray, he said to me, "Do the prayers and then they will become part of you." And even though I already had faith in God, I wasn't initially confident that God would see to it that I would keep both legs and walk with no canes. Rabbi Dresher told me to have faith. I said, "How do I have this kind of faith?"

He told me to do it and faith would follow. I remembered, "*Na'aseh ve-Neshma.*" He also said to me, "Douglas, if you sit in a chair, you don't worry about whether or not it will collapse. If you're driving a car, you don't worry that the engine will fall out. You have faith in the chair. You have faith in the car. And if you have faith in a chair that it will support you, should you not have faith in God that He will heal you? Doesn't common sense and intuition tell us that God has greater credibility than a wooden chair?" His argument was very persuasive.

Furthermore, Rabbi Dresher said to me, "It is within the Biblical tradition to negotiate a deal with God. Abraham did it. Moses did it. Job definitely tried." He told me to write a contract with God, to make a deal with God. He said to pray with unquestioning faith for three months. And if I noticed no amelioration of my physical disability, I could scrap this kind of "faithful prayer." But, if I saw practical results, this would be an indication that God and I were connecting, and that I was on my way to recovery.

I followed the rabbi's advice, and the faith that my mother planted in me grew even stronger. I learned that, like any other art, faith is a discipline that has to be practiced and that faith is not given to us by grace, but must be struggled for and fought for and worked for. Here is the irony and paradox I have discovered: Faith is ninety-nine percent perspiration and one percent inspiration.

One of my favorite commentaries to the Torah was written by Levi Yitzchak of Berdichev, a renowned eighteenth-century Hasidic leader. His popularity among the Hasidic Jewish people is surpassed only by the legendary Ba'al Shem Tov. He wrote a mystical explanation of the Torah called *Kedushat Levi*. I am particularly fond of his commentary to Parashat Yitro, the section of the Torah that deals with the Ten Commandments. (Exodus 18–20:23) In this section, *Kedushat Levi* emphasizes that faith in God is an art or discipline that must be practiced. He identifies faith with the Hebrew term *Mochin de-Gadlut*, which can be translated as "Greater Mind" or "Heightened Consciousness." When we don't have absolute faith that God will come through, we are then involved in *Mochin de-Katnut*, which may be translated as "Lesser Mind" or "Reduced Consciousness."

These Hebrew terms or concepts are derived from sixteenth-century Palestinian Kabbalistic thought, where they served to illustrate the changing religious modes in the ongoing life of every person. *Kedushat Levi* takes these terms and applies them to a person's faith. For example, pretend your brother has open heart surgery. During the surgery, you pray part of the time with faith that God will pull him through. Then a little later, you pray with fear that he might die. You are experiencing alternate states of faithful practice as you pray for your brother.

When my wife had cancer in 1996, if I prayed with fear that she would be ridden with the disease, I was praying with the Reduced State of Mind. Or, if I felt that Peggy might not be cured, or that it was God's will that she suffer for a greater purpose, I would also be praying with the Lesser State of Mind. But, when I prayed, and I did, knowing that Peggy would indeed be cured, and prayed with full confidence and surety that her healing had already begun, I was praying with the Heightened State of Mind. The transformative process from Reduced State to Heightened State is the key to successful prayer and to faith.

When we serve God with the Heightened Mind or with faith, we do not fear events that befall us. This does not mean that we are oblivious to tragedy. It means that our faith guides us. If we serve with the Reduced State of Mind, then we feel the fears and all the distresses that surround us. Our heart, our mind, our soul dwells in fear, and our lack of faith impedes successful prayer.

Levi Yitzchak maintains that when the Jews were in Egypt as slaves, they were a ragtag people with a slave mentality serving God with the Reduced Mind. Then Moses preached to them the concept of the Heightened Mind, *Mochin de-Gadlut*. He told each Jewish household to take a lamb, tie it to their beds, and tell the Egyptians that they were going to offer sacrifices of their lambs. The Hebrew response was, "Can we sacrifice that which is holy to the Egyptians and not be killed by them?" The ancient Israelites were terrified. They were governed by fear. But Moses taught them to abandon fear and embrace the Greater Mind. The people did this.

Kedushat Levi maintains that this was the Great Miracle. The Great Miracle was not the Splitting of the Sea or the Ten Plagues. The miraculous was not an external event. It was an internal event, an internal transformation in the mind and soul of every Israelite from the Reduced Mind to the Heightened Mind. Faith is the result of the transformative state that takes place within us.

This transformative process is not an easy internal dynamic. Initially, a person's faith is not as strong as it becomes after months and months of practice. I understand from my own experience, though, that the best way to achieve faith is to act with faith. As the ancient Israelites said, *Na'aseh ve-Neshma*. "Let us do it, then we will understand it." The second universal principle is Faith: Do it and faith will follow.

Liberating Concept: I can learn to have faith

MELINDA   Once Rabbi Douglas said that he believes that God does not want for us to suffer, my next step was faith. The movement from a view of God as a punishing parent to that of God as a force of love in the universe was easy. Learning faith was harder.

Rabbi Douglas's faith was stunning and his words were beautiful. As he told me the story of his own healing and that of others, he worked to "lend" me some of his faith. But even though the stories and words were moving and helped to break down some of my emotional barriers, they were not enough. One cannot will oneself to believe.

Every week I would come to see him and say things like, "I have to see this work in order to believe it." Once I compared myself to the Apostle Thomas from the Gospel of St. John. Rabbi Douglas went to his bookshelf, got down the New Testament, and asked me to find the verse. Thumbing through, I noticed that the book was well worn and many passages were underlined.

The expression "doubting Thomas" comes from an event that took place after Jesus had risen from the dead. Jesus had appeared to all of the apostles except Thomas. When Thomas was told that Jesus had risen from the dead, he replied: "Unless I see the mark of the nails in his hands, and put my finger in the mark of the nails and my hand in his side, I will not believe." (John 20:25) In order to believe, Thomas had to stick his finger into the palm of Jesus' hand. Good old Thomas decided that only the ultimate concrete evidence would convince him. (I often say that Thomas is a man after my own heart.) When they met, Jesus understood and compassionately told Thomas, "Put your finger here and see my hands. Reach out your hand and put it in my side. Do not doubt but believe." (John 20:27) And Thomas believed.

What I came to understand from this story is that, given the way that our human brains work, the best way for most of us to come to believe something is by experiencing it concretely. Most of us have what I call "our poor human brains," which means that often our intense desire to understand and to know goes far beyond what our minds are capable of.

I realized that for me, seeing is believing. Or better, experiencing is believing. Again, *accepting this idea was enormously liberating.* I could have faith if every day I did certain things and then experienced the results. I could *do* something!

So Rabbi Douglas taught me to "Do it and faith will follow" or as I like to say, "Fake it 'til you make it." Once I had learned the prayer and experienced the healing, my faith and trust in God began to grow. I also learned from my own experience that we don't come to have faith all at once—faith grows or is developed in small pieces.

During my early learning with Rabbi Douglas, I re-read the Four Gospels (figuring maybe I had missed something as a youth if this rabbi still reads them). I started with no small amount of defensiveness—I remembered a God of punishment for my childhood sins. But this time I saw in these pages an enormously compassionate Jesus healing the sick to build people's faith! He began his public life healing "those afflicted with various diseases and racked with pain; the possessed, the lunatics, and the paralyzed. He cured them all." (Matthew 4:5) I counted twenty-four instances of Jesus' healing in the Gospel of Matthew alone.

And Jesus healed with great compassion. It hurt him when he saw suffering, and he healed without judgment. He didn't care if the suffering person was Jewish or non-Jewish, a follower or even a sinner! Basically, that's what the whole thing was about. Jesus healed so people would then have faith in God. The healing and the teaching of faith were for everyone.

This sounded suspiciously familiar to me. The next time I saw Rabbi Douglas, I described this Jesus as very different from the one of my childhood. Rabbi Douglas smiled and said, with a twinkle in his eye, "It is always good to read the original sources. These are universal principles."

I learned to have faith. I had suffered from ovarian cysts for a year and the healing and faith worked for me. When, after a few weeks of saying the prayer as the Rabbi taught, the pain began to go away, I went into his office and exclaimed, "There is a God!" Rabbi Douglas answered, with a smile, "I know."

This is the Liberating Concept contained in the New Testament and in the way to faith taught in this book: *When we get answers to our prayers, our faith grows.*

There is a very simple formula for learning faith. You first decide what to pray for. Next, you pray a special prayer (see page 59) with *kavvanah*. And as you begin to be healed, a small piece of faith *clicks in*. You can almost physically feel the cognitive/mental/emotional click of a piece of faith.

To really make this work, you need to pray for specific answers to life problems or for specific things, including physical healing. Then it is very clear when the prayer is answered! There are many meditations to help find answers. The first meditation Rabbi Douglas taught me was the Dream Angel Meditation. It has been almost five years now, and I still use it every night. The answers I have received have been way beyond what my "poor human brain" could come up with. It is a way of accessing the wisdom of the universe.

When Rabbi Douglas taught me the Dream Angel Meditation at the end of our very first meeting, he said, "Melinda, I know this sounds a bit odd, but you have to write the question and put it under your pillow. I don't know why it works that way and, again, I know it sounds a bit odd."

I approached this prayer with a "beginner's mind" never having done anything like this before in my life. Given my misery, this seemed like a new, different, fun thing to do. It gave me something to look forward to. Going to sleep became an adventure. You can use it to find out exactly what to pray for.

Using it for physical healing will be explained in chapter five. We also will discuss this meditation more when we explore emotional healing, as it is a particularly powerful way to access what is bothering us.

How to Do It

DREAM ANGEL MEDITATION

RABBI DOUGLAS   The Kabbalah teaches that we can use dreams to guide us in our healing. Rabbi Dresher taught me the concept of dream meditations, which are found in a thirteenth-century volume called *She'elot u-Teshuvot min ha-Shamayyim* (*Responsa from Heaven*) by Jacob Marvege. This particular dream meditation is a variation of what Rabbi Dresher taught me.

Before going to bed at night, write down on a small piece of paper a question that has been bothering you. The question should be very focused. (For example: "I feel very tired every day. What's causing this tiredness?")

Then recite the Hebrew *Shema* prayer, "Hear O Israel, the Lord our God, the Lord is One," again and again and again as a *mantra*. And, as you recite the *Shema*, visualize the Hebrew letters. If you don't know Hebrew, recite the *Shema* in English, "Hear O Israel, the Lord our God, the Lord is One," visualizing and focusing in on each letter, and reciting each word as a *mantra*.

Now, meditate on your question for about five minutes. Then recite this prayer, "Dream Angel, with the help of *Adonai*,[1] please visit me this night, and answer my question in my dream, by indicating to me a verse from Scripture or by speech or by a vision. And when I wake up, let me understand your message so that I will know what to do."

Please do write your question on a piece of paper. This question should be written *before* you do this Dream Angel Meditation, as mentioned above. After you have said the prayer, put the piece of paper under your pillow. Do this for several days. You will have a dream. A vivid dream. It may be symbolic or it may be very literal.

Let me say when you practice this meditation, if you are very "wiped out" upon retiring, it won't work. Obviously you will be tired upon retiring, but it is important to think clearly and be able to focus clearly. If you do this, you will receive a response. And many of you will receive direction on what exactly to pray for.

3: THE GREATER MIND

Universal Principle: The Greater Mind

RABBI DOUGLAS   FAITH, to me, is a state of mind. To pray effectively, we must pray with faith. Rabbi Arthur Green's essay, "Teachings of the Hasidic Masters," is what first directed me to the Hebrew text of *Kedushat Levi* by Rabbi Levi Yitzchak. *Kedushat Levi* has had a great influence on my life of prayer. As mentioned earlier, I was particularly moved by its commentary of Parashat Yitro (Exodus 18–20:23).

In his commentary on the First Commandment of the Ten Commandments ("I am the Lord Your God, who brought thee out of the land of Egypt, out of the house of bondage"), Levi Yitzchak discusses an important Jewish mystical concept: the idea of Greater and Lesser States of Mind that an individual has in the service of God. I have seen that when an understanding of these states of mind is applied to prayer, our prayers become enormously powerful. The Jewish mystical ideas of Greater and Lesser States of Mind not only allow us to understand how we can be brought closer to God through prayer, they also show us the importance of faith in prayer. The Hebrew Kabbalistic words *Mochin de-Katnut* (Lesser Mind) and *Mochin de-Gadlut* (Greater Mind) illustrate and contrast how a person prays when he or she is in an ordinary state of mind as opposed to a state of mind that is filled with faith.

Rabbi Yitzchak says,

Everyone who serves God with the Greater Mind has no fear and trepidation of any events that may happen to him. Even though he may appear to be in trouble, he has no fear in his mind and in his heart that any harm will befall him. You only assume that he has distress. However, he who serves God with the Lesser Mind fears all the events that happen to him, in his mind and in his heart, he feels fear. Because of this, external forces overpower him and he is under their domain.

Those who serve God with the Greater Mind are not afraid of difficult situations that may befall them, such as illness or financial loss or loss of a child. People who have the Greater Mind are impervious to external circumstances and put complete trust in God, knowing that God will be with them and never abandon them.

Rabbi Levi Yitzchak recognizes that this is no easy feat. He quotes from Psalm 118 the agonizing moments of King David, who vacillated between moments influenced by the Greater Mind and moments under the domain of the Lesser Mind. In this Psalm, King David is beset by his enemies. The Psalm shows the king's fear of failure one day and his sureness of success another day.

All of us climb up and down the Ladder of Faith. All of us are subject to moments of Greater and Lesser Faith, like King David. But, when we pray, we should strive to pray with faith, with the Greater Mind. This must be our goal.

As mentioned earlier, *Kedushat Levi* teaches that the miraculous is not an external event; it is an internal one, a faithful commitment to an idea in a person's soul, or an internal transformation. Levi Yitzchak taught that the people of Israel, even though they were in bondage in Egypt, achieved an inner transformation that preceded their physical freedom. This inner dynamic was the radical change of each individual from the Lesser Mind to the Greater Mind. The slave mentality gave way to the free mentality. This happened because of faith, and a person has faith when his or her life is lived in the Greater Mind. Here is a key passage from the text:

This is why the commentators wrote that the Sabbath preceding Passover should be called The Great Sabbath (*Shabbat Hagadol*). This is because of the great miracle that happened before the first

Passover in Egypt. On the tenth of the month, they set aside their lambs and they tied them to the bed posts. When the Egyptians asked why they were doing this, they replied that "We must slaughter them since God commanded us to do so." The Egyptians became furious because of this, for they considered these lambs to be their gods. They called this miracle more great than the rest of the miracles. Were there not greater miracles than this miracle? Was not the splitting of the Red Sea or the rest of the miracles that the Lord did with His people Israel greater than this miracle? The secret is that here we are taught that Israel at that time was serving God with the Greater Mind. Now, whoever serves God with the Greater Mind, has no fear of whatever may befall him, as we have explained above. And it is in this context that the commentators called this THE GREAT MIRACLE. The Miracle of the Greater Mind. [The miracle was that] they had no fear of the Egyptians even though they desired to slaughter the Egyptian gods. Also, we understand that on the tenth of the month, they took these lambs, tied them to the beds and told the Egyptians that they wished to slaughter the Passover sacrifice. Just before this, they had said, "If we sacrifice that which is untouchable to the Egyptians before their very eyes, will they not stone us!" (Exodus 8:22) The Biblical text says, "before their very eyes." They were afraid of the Egyptians because they were always watching them. But just as we explained earlier, that since they entered into the levels of Greater Mind, they did not focus on the Egyptians watching them, because they were in a high state. They had no fear of anything and the rule of Egypt and their power were not considered, and it is possible to say that, because of this, God commanded them that they take the lambs on the tenth day of the month in order to bring them into the state of the Greater Mind. . . .

This is the meaning of Jethro's prayer "Blessed be the Lord, who delivered you from the Egyptians and from Pharaoh, and who delivered the people from under the hand of the Egyptians." (Exodus 18: 10–11) This prayer refers to the Great Miracle by which they were delivered from their troubles. But, "who delivered the people from under the hand of the Egyptians" shows that God, in great love for His believers, while they were still in Egypt, emanated upon them an emanation so that they could serve Him with the Greater Mind. And with this, they came forth from under the hand of Egypt in that they no longer bowed to them and they no longer feared them.

The text, "Now I know that the Lord is great" means that now they serve God with the Greater Mind.

Another example of the Greater Mind is the story of Elijah the Prophet. Jewish people all over the world recognize the greatness and the mystique of Elijah, ninth century mystic/prophet of Israel. Elijah resided in ancient Gilead, but we do not have exact information where he was born. Holy Scripture refers to him as the Tishbite of Tishby in Gilead; perhaps he was born in Tishby of Naphtale.

What is important for us is that Elijah is the most mystical person of the Hebrew Scriptures. He passed into immortal life without going through death. His disciple, Elisha, was given a gift almost as great: He saw his teacher depart soul and body into the heavens, and he also received the mantle which was possibly the channel of Elijah's power.

Elijah has become such a powerful mystical figure in Jewish custom that the Jewish family sets aside a special chair for Elijah at every circumcision (*bris*), and a separate cup of wine is poured for Elijah at every Passover table. According to Jewish tradition, it is Elijah who will announce the coming of the Messiah. Elijah is present to all Jews, young and old. He was the intercessor of the Jewish people. He challenged God, thanked God, and praised God. He was a man of God. Even the Talmudic rationalists revere him. When an argument remains unsolved in Talmud, the Talmudic doctors claim that Elijah will solve the problem at the end of days. One day, Elijah will come back to earth, and he will solve all contradictions, all conflicts, all disagreements. He will usher in an era of healing and peace.

This mystic Elijah was a healer in his own time, in his own land. "And the word of the Lord came to him: 'Go at once to Zarephath of Sidon, and stay there; I have designated a widow there to feed you.'"

(I Kings 17:8–9) Now, it happened in that town that a widow befriended Elijah. Even though she had minimal food and drink, she extended hospitality to him. While Elijah was staying in her home, the widow's son became gravely ill. The Scripture says, "'Give me the boy,' he said to her; and taking him from her arms, he carried him to the upper chamber where he was staying, and laid him down on his own bed. He cried out to the Lord and said, 'O Lord my God, will You bring calamity upon this widow whose guest I am, and let her son die?' Then he stretched out over the child three times, and cried out to the Lord, saying, 'O Lord my God, let this child's life return to his body!' The Lord heard Elijah's plea; the child's life returned to his body, and he revived." (I Kings 17:19–22)

The Hebrew *Midrash*,[1] *Tanna Debe Eliyyahu*, elaborates on the teachings of the school of thought that bears Elijah's name. The text maintains that Elijah was able to heal the son of the woman of Zarephath "because he did the will of Him at whose word the world came into being—the Holy One blessed be He. And because every day without fail, he voiced his anguish that the Holy One had withdrawn His Glory from Israel, and that the Glory of Israel was gone; indeed, it seemed to him as though Israel—may such an end befall its enemies—was about to perish from the world."

Elijah's healing was so great that he brought the dead boy back to life. This midrash maintains that Elijah was able to heal because "he did the will of Him." That is, he identified completely with God. And he did this by entering into the state of the Greater Mind.

Elijah's ability to do this is clearly illustrated when Elijah was hiding in a cave from the wicked Queen Jezebel. The Lord said to Elijah, "'Why are you here Elijah?' He replied: 'I am moved by zeal for the Lord, the God of Hosts, for the Israelites have forsaken Your covenant, torn down Your altars, and put Your prophets to the sword. I alone am left, and they are out to take my life.' 'Come out,' He called, 'and stand on the mountain before the Lord.' And lo, the Lord passed by. There was a great and mighty *wind*, splitting mountains and shattering rocks by the power of the Lord; but the Lord was not in the wind. After the *wind*—an *earthquake;* but the Lord was not in the *earthquake*. After the *earthquake*—a *fire;* but the Lord was not in the *fire;* and after the *fire; a Still Small Voice.* When Elijah heard it, he wrapped his mantle about his face and went out and stood at the entrance of the cave." (I Kings 19: 9–13)

Just as King David had greater and lesser moments of faith, so did Elijah. Nevertheless, Elijah recognized that the miraculous, his finding God, did not happen in a windstorm or in a strong earthquake, or even in a terrible fire. The voice of God that Elijah searched for was not found in an external event, but it was found in an internal event that happened within the soul of Elijah.

Elijah entered the cave with fear and trembling and shared with the Lord his terrifying anxiety: "Because the Israelites have forsaken your Covenant; torn down your altars, and put your prophets to the sword. I alone am left, and they are out to take my life." It is at this point that God commands Elijah to *listen.* Elijah is fearful, anxious, and angry with his people. He is unable to hear the word of God because he is in a state of Lesser Mind, *Mochin de-Katnut.* But then, he has an intuition, and his intuition encourages him to try again to really hear the word of God. So Elijah looks outward at the external events that happen all around him—wind, fire, earthquake. God cannot be found. It is only when Elijah recognizes that the Lord is found *within,* that he *hears* the Voice of God.

It is at this point that Elijah's faith is so great that he recognizes the God within him, and he enters into *Mochin de-Gadlut,* the state of Greater Mind. And the miracle that took place with Elijah on the mount was not the great fire or earthquake or powerful wind. It was none of these external events. Nor was the miracle the *Still Small Voice* of God. But the true miracle was an internal transformation within Elijah, a transformative process from Elijah's Lesser Mind to Greater Mind.

Elijah's disciple, Elisha, was also a prophet. When Elijah experienced his remarkable vision at Mount Horub, including the embracing of the Still Small Voice and entering into the state of the Greater Mind, he again replied to the Lord, "I am moved by zeal for the Lord, the God of Hosts; for the Israelites have forsaken Your covenant, torn down Your altars, and have put Your prophets to the sword. I alone am left, and they are out to take my life." (I Kings 19:14)

This time God answers in a most stoic manner: "Anoint Elisha, son of Shaphat of Abel-Meholah to succeed you as prophet." (I Kings 19:16) What God means is, "I guess you're right. Consequently we need a new prophet to take over your ministry and he shall be Elisha." God's answer is amazing! One would think that God would console Elijah, but God is a very practical God. He and Elijah have already embraced in a Still Small Voice, and now it is time for the Lord to tell Elijah that his tenure among the Jews has come to an end and that it is time for Elisha to receive the mantle of spiritual power. Elisha, like Elijah, understood that to perceive and receive God, one has to enter into *Mochin de-Gadlut.*

The dialogue between the two prophets, I believe, is a metaphor for exchanging the Lesser Mind for the Greater Mind. The Scripture states that after God appeared to Elijah and instructed him to pass the mantle to Elisha, Elijah departed and found Elisha in a field. Elijah remembered God's command and threw Elisha his mantle. Elisha understood the significance of this act and immediately said to Elijah, "Let me kiss my father and my mother goodbye, and I will follow you." (I Kings 19:20) But, Elijah is disappointed that Elisha speaks in this manner because Elijah understands that when Elisha states that he wants to embrace his mother and father and then follow him, this means that Elisha is still in the world of the Lesser Mind, which ties him to his mother and father.

We can imagine Elijah responding, "You don't understand the significance of my throwing the mantle. You missed the significance of our meeting and our relationship. With my throwing the mantle, I am inviting you to leave the Lesser Mind and enter the Greater Mind. You don't need to associate with your mother and father. Identify with me." Elijah clearly maintains that you can't live in the Greater and Lesser Mind simultaneously. You must choose, and with Perfect Faith, "one leaves his mother and father, one leaves the Lesser Mind and embraces the Greater Mind."

After Elisha has been instructed in the Greater Mind, he encounters a Shunammite woman and her son. "One day Elisha visited Shunem. A wealthy woman lived there, and she urged him to have a meal; and whenever he passed by, he would stop there for a meal. Once she said to her husband, 'I am sure it is a holy man of God who comes this way regularly.'" (II Kings 4:8–9) The Shunammite woman then consults with her husband and they agree to create for Elisha a wonderful roof-top apartment with a bed, a table, a stove, and a candlestick. Elisha in gratitude asks the woman, through his servant, "How can I thank you? What can I do for you?" She is vague, giving no direct answer. And so Elisha again asks his servant, Gehazi, "What can I do for the Shunammite woman?"

Gehazi answers, "The woman's husband is old and she still has no child." Then Elisha says to his servant, "Call her. . . . He called her, and she stood in the doorway. And Elisha said, 'At this season next year, you will be embracing a son.' . . . The woman conceived and bore a son at the same season the following year, as Elisha had assured her." (II Kings: 4:15–17)

Here the prophet Elisha knew immediately that the Shunammite woman would have a son. He has no doubts; he is confident in his faith that she will bear a child. Elisha did not pray with hesitancy. He did not say, "O God, let it be Thy will the Shunammite woman have a child." He did not waiver and doubt the efficacy of his vision. He became one with God. And, since he and God became one, he recognized that his will was God's will and God's will was his will. He recognized this because his absolute faith had brought him into a state of the Greater Mind. Just as Moses had said, "Let her be healed" with respect to Miriam's leprosy, Elisha said, "Thou shalt embrace a son." Both are prayerful statements articulated with absolute faith.

And one day, when the child was grown, he went out to work in the field with his father, and he suffered a severe headache. His father said to one of the servants, "Take the boy to his mother." The Shunammite woman, filled with fear and worry and fright, embraced her child as he sat on her knees. Tragically, he died. But now an amazing thing happened. The woman, instead of accepting the death of her son as the will of God, brought the boy to the prophet's newly furnished apartment. She could not accept that the death of her son was God's will. She had already seen the faith of Elisha. He had prophesized a son would be born. And a son was born. She knew, with intuitive knowledge that the God who allowed her son to be born, would not allow for him to die.

When she met Elisha, she was an ordinary woman with ordinary faith. But she saw Elisha's great faith, and I believe that this inspired in her an inner transformation from Lesser Mind to Greater Mind. She knew with the Greater Mind that it was God's will for her child to live, because in the state of the Greater Mind, her will is God's will and God's will is her will. And it was this faith that inspired her to search out Elisha. And, he saw her, and said to his servant, "Gehazi, ask how her family is doing—she, her husband, her child." And when Gehazi asks her about her child, she answers, "It is well." Her confidence is so strong that God will not let her son die. Her faith is so strong that, with the Greater Mind, she tells the servant, "All is well."

This was exactly what Rabbi Dresher taught me—that my vision at all times must be a vision of healing, and that my statements must at all times be positive and strong. For the Greater Mind does not allow for negative statements, even in the face of serious external circumstances. You have faith that God will lift you to safety. The Greater Mind teaches us that we thank God in advance of our cure, just as the Shunammite woman recognized that with her son, "All is well." She looked into the future and with the Greater Mind, she saw her boy well, and she said with her lips what she saw with her mind.

After a while, Elisha came into the house of the woman and into his apartment. And the dead child lay upon his bed. And the text says that Elisha shut the door of his apartment and lay on the child, offering him some sort of mouth-to-mouth resuscitation, but more than this—much more than this. He "put his mouth upon his mouth and his eyes upon his eyes, and his hands upon his hands and he stretched himself upon him; and the flesh of the child waxed warm." And consistent with the Biblical healing prayer of faith, he must have recited the prayer of Moses, "El Na Rifa Na La," (see pp. 59–60) as he shared his body with the child's body, allowing his body to be a tunnel of the Living God. Then Elisha took a break and walked around.

Notice how human and how real this Biblical story is. I know when I pray with an individual, I take breaks to refuel and replenish the light within me. That's why I recommend, when we pray for another, or pray for ourselves, we constantly see ourselves filled with the light of God. This is our fuel. This is our power. This is our God that is within us. And when we are healing another, or healing ourselves, it's important to take a break. And in this break, we can sing, remember a joke or two, and visualize ourselves once again filled with the light of God.

Then we do as Elisha did: We go back to the business of healing. "He stepped down, walked once up and down the room, then mounted and bent over him. Thereupon, the boy sneezed seven times, and the boy opened his eyes." (II Kings 4:35)

The miracle in this marvelous Biblical story is not only the healing of the child, nor is it only the story of this man of faith whose life was lived in the Greater Mind. The greatest of the miracles was the inner transformation that took place within the spirit and soul of the Shunammite woman—the inner transformation from Lesser Mind to Greater Mind. As the story unfolded, we saw an ordinary woman of ordinary faith. But as the story progresses, we see a remarkable woman with remarkable faith who upon seeing her son dead, said, "All is well." The greatest miracle in this miraculous story was her turn from fear of external circumstances to absolute faith in God, a transformative process from Lesser Mind to Greater Mind. Here we learn how the transformative process can occur in anyone and everyone.

HOW DO WE KNOW WHEN WE ARE IN THE GREATER MIND?

When I teach students about the Greater and Lesser Mind, or when I pray with people, encouraging them to be in the Greater Mind, they frequently ask, "Rabbi, how do I know if I am in the Greater Mind? How do I know what it feels like to be in the Greater Mind?"

When I pray with someone, I know that I am in the Greater Mind if I feel a great sense of joy, a feeling of being connected with God, and knowing that all will be alright. For example, I remember several months ago, a member of my synagogue came into my office. She told me she was in the early stages of MS. I felt sad for her. My heart went out to her. But, I realized I couldn't stay in this state. I then remembered the joy of Rabbi Nachman of Bratslav. I remembered the faith of Rabbi Levi Yitzchak of Berdichev. I remembered the words of the Ba'al Shem Tov who said, "One must believe that as soon as the prayer has been said, the person is answered for what he has prayed for." And I felt a change from sadness to joy. This recognition of the transformative process from sadness to joy was my signal that I was in the Greater Mind.

Several years ago, I prayed with a woman with severe emphysema, with tubes going into her nostrils, carrying oxygen from her oxygen tanks. She was a very bitter person who was not only indifferent to God, but considered her atheism a religion. As much as I tried, I was unable to maintain a joyous state. As much as I tried, and I did try to pray with faith and joy, it was as if I were forcing it too strongly. She continued to do everything her doctors told her not to do, like sneaking cigarettes. I knew in my heart that, in this instance, I was unable to pray with the Greater Mind. There was no overwhelming sense of happiness and faith when we met together.

When you are praying in the Lesser Mind, you have fear of events that may befall you. When my wife Peggy was diagnosed with cancer—at that moment, I felt as though I had received a punch in the stomach, and I thought that perhaps Peggy was going to die. I felt terrified and sad for her and for me, and I felt so unconnected with God. This was the Lesser Mind.

As long as I was in the Lesser Mind, my prayers could not be successful. It did not matter how hard I prayed or for how long I prayed. Since I was not in the Greater Mind, my prayers could not succeed. Fear of what will happen, fear of outside circumstances are the strongest indicators that you are praying in the Lesser Mind.

It was only a few days later, when I visited the Holy Ark of our synagogue, and stood in front of the *Sifrei Torah* (scrolls) in the Ark, feeling the grandeur of God, remembering how God put me and Peggy together (we met on a Tuesday, considered a special day for blessing in the Jewish faith). I always knew God was our matchmaker.

As I stood in front of the Ark, visualizing Peggy, I felt a transformative process taking place within me—the fear that had surrounded me for two days was replaced by the surety that God would pull Peggy out of this quagmire of cancer. This internal dynamic that took place within me, this change from fear to faith, placed me in the midst of the Greater Mind. I knew I was in the Greater Mind. When you feel a transformative process within you, a change from sadness to joy, you know you're in the Greater Mind.

Last summer, Peggy and I received a telephone call from my mother-in-law, Shirley Bagley. She told us that her husband Bill had suffered a stroke which had exacerbated his Parkinson's Disease. We flew down to be with them. When I saw Bill in the nursing home, he did not look like the robust golfer I had known for the past eighteen years. He couldn't walk. He was very incoherent, and he was hallucinating.

In my prayers for him, I began to visualize him well and healthy, swinging his golf club on the greens. I tried to pray with faith that God had already cured him. I tried to visualize him and his golfing buddies, but the vision didn't happen. As much as I tried to see light, I saw darkness. As much as I tried to see Bill playing golf, I saw Bill lying in bed, writhing in pain. As much as I wanted God to cure him, I intuitively felt that God wanted to take him and heal him in a spiritual way, but not in a physical way.

My inability to visualize my father-in-law well, even though I tried so hard, was a clear indication to me that I was in the Lesser Mind. I was only able to pray with the Greater Mind when I accepted that my father-in-law was not going to become physically better. In this instance, the Greater Mind took on a transformative process from Fear of Death to Acceptance of Death.

When I looked back on this experience, I realized that sometimes we think that our prayers are not accepted, and we feel blue and sad. And yet, it is only that the effect of our prayers are in the celestial world of the universe and not in the material world. So, sometimes, our prayers appear to be in vain. But that's only in *this* world, not in the heavenly world.

When I struggled and fought and didn't understand why, I remained in the Lesser Mind. I was afraid, I was unable to visualize, I was discouraged, and my faith was not strong. It was as if I fell down the Ladder of Faith. It was only after my father-in-law had died that we felt that he was now reunited with God. And then, I had a vision of him playing golf in the heavenly world. This visual metaphor strengthened my love for God and inspired in me this change from sadness to inner peace, and even joy. Dad was no longer suffering. I knew I was now in the Greater Mind and I was thrilled.

The Ba'al Shem Tov said what I was thinking when I was in the Lesser Mind. "False humility causes man to think that his service of God, his prayers and Torah, are of no importance. Actually, one must understand that he is a ladder set on the earth and its top reaches into the heavens—that is, all his motions, his speech, his behavior, his participations, affect the uppermost realms." When I realized this insight of the Ba'al Shem Tov, I experienced again the Greater Mind.

Many years ago I had a wonderful friendship with a deaf Catholic man. My congregation is a congregation of deaf and hearing people. I teach and preach, using speech and sign language. Since we are the only deaf house of worship in the northern suburbs of Chicago, one of our frequent visitors was a deaf Catholic man named Louis.

Louis used to visit me at least once a week, and we had the most wonderful theological conversations. He believed that God lives within us and the more Godly we act to one another, the more powerful God becomes. Louis was a carpenter, and such a gentle kind human being that he built our first Ark—where the Torahs are kept—for free. But most importantly, Louis had more faith in God than any person I had ever met. His faith inspired me so much. I even felt that he was sent by God to inspire my faith when it wavered.

One day some thugs firebombed his apartment. It was a hate crime against the deaf. He was rushed to St. Francis Hospital. I visited him regularly. Several weeks later, I received a telephone call from the hospital at about 1 A.M. The nurse told me that Louis was

in a coma, and his family had requested that I perform Last Rites.
Since I am not a Catholic, I called my very dear friend Father Joe.
Father Joe is the most hard-working and kindest clergyman I know,
and I asked him to meet me at the hospital so he could do the Last
Rites. Joe accepted the call and we met at the hospital in Evanston.

We went into Louis' room—there were nurses, family members,
several doctors, now joined by a priest and a rabbi. They told us he
was dying. And then immediately, I told Joe not to do the Last Rites.
Instead, I asked Joe to climb on a chair and remove the Cross from
the wall.

I told Joe that if he held the Cross in front of Louis, Louis would
wake up. As a rabbi, and a committed Jew, I felt too uncomfortable
holding the Cross. That's why I asked Joe to do it. But rather than
remove the Cross, Joe compassionately put his arm around me and
tried to get me to accept Louis' imminent death.

But, I knew Louis would not die. I was confident that if we showed
him the Cross, he would somehow break out of the coma. I got up on
the chair and removed the Cross myself. I placed it in Louis' hands,
and he awoke. And instantly, the nurse said to me with a smile, "Well
Rabbi, do you want to convert?"

"No," I said. I didn't convert. I remained a faithful Jew, because I
recognized that the power of the Cross to a faithful Christian is as
important as is the power of the Torah to a faithful Jew. Faith is for
everyone. I knew that the Cross in Louis' hands would give him life.
I knew this because I was in the Greater Mind. And I knew I was in
the Greater Mind because, at that moment, my faith in God, and in
God's saving power was as strong and as real as the air I was breathing. In addition, the mental image I had of Louis sitting up and smiling
and signing to me was as clear and crisp as the reality of the people
around me. My faith reminded me of the great enormous faith that
Louis had in his Cross. And my Greater Mind reminded me that when
one's faith is so great, the most amazing things can happen!

It was as if God was speaking to me, actually. God was speaking
to me. And I heard His voice and without hesitancy, I went for it.
This is being in the Greater Mind.

Liberating Concept: The Greater Mind for me!

MELINDA   When Rabbi Douglas first told me about "the Greater
                 Mind," I said to myself: "Yeah, right. That's not possi-
ble. Just look at me—a mess of fear and doubt." Now, what seemed
impossible several years ago is becoming part of me.

Seeing the prayer work leads to faith, and faith leads to the Greater
Mind, a surety of God. This is a process like any other skill-building.
If you have ever done any physical training, this works the same—you
feel the strength gradually develop and then, one day, you can do
something you have never been able to do before! At a specific moment
I knew that I had experienced the Greater Mind and it was thrilling
and liberating.

My siblings and I (all eight of us) keep in touch via E-mail. Not
long ago, an E-mail from my sister, Mary Anne, said that she had
found a lump on her neck and the doctor had ordered a thyroid test.
The lump was large enough that she had felt it while casually touch-
ing her neck. The doctor felt it, too. The news hit me like a stab in
the heart. If the blood test came back elevated, it meant an overactive
thyroid. Then what she had felt was probably part of the thyroid and
producing the hormones. But if it came back normal, it meant a tumor.

The test came back normal. Mary Anne's next E-mail read, "I am
sure that whatever is there will need to come out. I was talking to Ellen,
and she said her friend had the same thing. Hers was malignant and
they removed the thyroid. I will have an isotope test next Monday."

Of the eight children, Mary Anne and I are the closest in age (six-
teen months apart) and the only two girls. As children, we depended
on each other through many rough years. As adults, we have renewed
that closeness. My first reaction to the E-mail was fear and anxiety. I
woke up every half hour at night. It took a couple of days to settle
down to pray. That is when the internal miracle occurred in me, just
as it had in the people of Israel.

In the past something like this would have filled me with worry
and fear. Not this time! As I began praying, there was a certainty in
me that Mary Anne's thyroid would be clear the day of the test. I

remember being startled by the knowledge—doing a double take during the prayer—and saying to myself, "Wow, this is new!" This was the Greater Mind. It is one of the ways to hear the "Voice of God."

Lest the psychiatric diagnoses start pouring in, the voice is not actually "heard." We have all had the experience of intuition—a sudden, strong, clear knowing that something is right or true. Recall the experience of intuition and it will take you close to what the Greater Mind feels like. Now add joy and you will be even closer to what the Greater Mind feels like. Remember: *sudden, strong, clear and joyful!*

(The Voice of God can be "heard" in different ways, too. The Voice of God can be intuition that comes during or after prayer and/or meditation. In difficult situations now I pray for guidance, refilling myself with light. As a result, I often find myself saying or doing things that I had not really known I was going to say or do—and the results are fantastic! Often, the day after doing the Dream Angel Meditation, an answer will come to me. It will be, again, an answer that is sudden, strong, and clear and makes perfect sense. The sensation will be: "Oh, of course!")

The Greater Mind brings inner peace. As Paul Brunton, an English philosopher and mystic, wrote in his *Notebooks:*

> He who knows and feels the divine power in his inmost being will be set free in the most literal sense of the word from anxieties and cares. He who has not yet arrived at this stage but is on the way to it can approach the same desirable result by the intensity of his faith in that being. But such a one must really have the faith and not merely say so. The proof that he possesses it would lie in the measure with which he refuses to accept negative thoughts, fearful thoughts, despondent thoughts. In the measure that he does not fail in his faith and hence in his thinking, in that measure, the higher power will not fail to support him in his hour of need. This is why Jesus told his disciples, "Take no anxious thought for the morrow."

So there was one week to pray for Mary Anne. This became a "prayer project," as Agnes Sanford would say. I encouraged Mary Anne to visualize herself well and to say, "Thank you God for having healed me" throughout the day. I e-mailed a close friend and asked for her prayers. I called Rabbi Douglas and he said he would pray. I brought Mary Anne's picture to the prayer group. As a group, during the beginning meditation, we focused on what a magnificent thing we were all doing, being partners with God for this healing. We concentrated on praying with joy and felt the great power of group prayer. We applied what Agnes Sanford knew when she wrote: "Just believing a set of facts about God does not necessarily turn on the power in a single one of our prayer-objectives. In order to do that, we must believe that we are receiving the thing that we desire. If we really believe this, we will naturally rejoice and give thanks for it. And when our belief is weak, the act of rejoicing and giving thanks will awaken our faith."

The most powerful prayer is done by those who love the person prayed for—and that meant me! I prayed with my husband, Jim, every day and then a second time by myself later in the day. There certainly were times when I prayed with more *kavvanah* and joy than others, but I prayed anyway. Throughout the day, I worked to keep a picture of a healthy Mary Anne in my mind, filled with light, and I thanked God for having healed her.

You might say that this is more energy than you have. But think about it—what are the stakes here? This is my sister. I called upon God to answer my prayer.

The goal is to move from prayer motivated by worry and fear to a prayer with deepening experience of the Presence of God—the joy, awe, peace that come with experiencing the Presence of God.[2]

My goal was to keep Mary Anne in my mind all day, seeing her well and saying, "Thank you God for having healed Mary Anne." This constant awareness comes with practice.

Now, was I calm on the Monday of the isotope test? Yes and no. My faith told me she would be well; my heart pounded. At 5 P.M. Mary Anne called and I held my breath. She said that the test had found nothing. Her thyroid was clear! The doctor could not even feel anything on examination! We both started crying. I cried with relief for her and joy in God.

I told Mary Anne that this was really wonderful for her, of course, and it also was wonderful for me. This time my prayers had been different. My faith was different. I had been able to visualize her well. I was in the Greater Mind. I told her that my only doubt had been in my ability, that my prayer would not work so quickly because I am still learning and am not a "master." She replied, "Well, you may not be a master yet but you are definitely in an AP (Advanced Placement) class." I burst out laughing.

More and more my spiritual movement since starting this work has been in the direction Paul Brunton writes so eloquently about when he discusses the Long Path and the Short Path. In the "Long Path," one must do the work of the spiritual exercises and self-improvement. Then in the "Short Path" one must be aware of God at all times and in all things. Both practices are essential. The ultimate goal is to "remember to live in the rarefied atmosphere of the Overself [*i.e.*, Greater Mind] instead of worrying about the ego and measuring its spiritual development. You learn to trust more and more in the Higher Power." To me, this passage is amazing. Here is a twentieth-century British philosopher echoing the Hebrew mystic Levi Yitzchak. These principles are universal and for everyone!

This practice of keeping God with us all day and striving for faith, the Greater Mind, is rooted in a universal principle that has been in every source I have come across. Brunton quotes it from Krishna in the Bhagavad Gita, a gospel of Hinduism considered one of the world's greatest religious classics: "The student must place this seed-thought in his mind and hold to it throughout the day. He need not fear that he will lose anything material thereby. Let him remember the definite promise of the Overself speaking through Krishna in the Bhagavad Gita: 'I look after the interests and safety of those who are perpetually engaged on My service, and whose thoughts are always about Me and Me alone.' He will learn by direct experience the literal meaning of the term Providence—'that which provides.'"

When one is in the state of the Greater Mind, one is not afraid. Not only is there so much in everyday life to be afraid of, but many of us carry a terrible, generalized fear from traumas in childhood.

When one learns early and intensely that the world is not a safe, nurturing place, the fear stays and festers. Fear is the greatest disabler. Faith and joy are the best enablers. Even though emotional healing is more difficult than physical healing, it can happen. (See chapter 6.)

How to Do It

Spiritual exercise to reach the Greater Mind

RABBI DOUGLAS 1. Choose a place that will become your regular place of meditation. Do this meditation every day at about the same time. This will ensure a sense of stability, constancy, and comfort. Sit in a comfortable chair or, if you wish, you may lie down.

2. Close your eyes. Do not cross your arms or legs. Take a deep breath through your nose and imagine the breath flowing to your brain, throughout your body, down to your toes and up again to your nostrils, when you exhale. Do this three times.

3. Repeat these words, either out loud or to yourself: "I am a wonderful human being. I am unique in creation. I transcend all ordinary thinking and dwell entirely in the Greater Mind."

4. Take a deep breath through your nose and again imagine the breath flowing to your brain, throughout your body, down to your toes and up again to your nostrils, when you exhale. Do this three times.

5. Repeat the following words three times: "I am in the Greater Mind. In the Greater Mind, I am one with God. My will can do anything."

This spiritual exercise allows you to move from the Lesser Mind to the Greater Mind. This contact will make the power of the Greater Mind available to you.

4: PRACTICING THE PRESENCE
OF GOD

Universal Principle: Prayer is an art
that must be practiced

RABBI DOUGLAS   As WE learn with the Candle Meditation, the Presence of God is not found by searching the heavens. The Presence of God also is not found only by making pilgrimages or visiting holy places or sitting by sacred persons. The Presence of God is within us.

The wonderful Psalm 139—which the Jewish people recite at the end of the Yom Kippur service, a highly spiritual day for us—illustrates most clearly where God is: "Whither I flee from Thy spirit, or whither I flee from Thy presence, if I send up into the heaven, Thou art there. If I make my bed in the netherworld, Thou art there. If I take the wings of the morning and dwell in the uttermost parts of the sea, even there, shall Thy hand lead me, and Thy right hand shall hold me." (Psalm 139, 7–10) Where we are, God is; where God is, we are, because we are one, inseparable and indivisible.

It is a universal principle that one must practice the Presence of God if one is to activate the God within us. One practices the Presence of God through prayer. If you do not practice praying, then the prayers cannot be efficacious. In order to be a good "pray-er" (the noun: a person who prays), you have to practice. Prayer is an art. When we do this, we can learn how to touch God. We must invite God within us. Reaching God is as much an art as playing the violin or hitting baseballs.

God is found within ùs. And God is found within us at the moment of birth, whether we are baptized or circumcised, whether we are Hindu, Jew, Moslem, atheist, Christian, Quaker, or whatever. God is the essence of our heart and soul.

However, we humans must increase the God within us. We do this through the Candle Meditation. We humans must turn God on. We must activate God. We must connect with the God that is within us, if we want to receive Her/His healing Presence.

My experience with God teaches me that God is a being or force like electricity. And we humans are wired for this "electricity." The spark of God is always within us at birth, but it is up to us to energize ourselves with God. It is up to us to fill ourselves up with God, by allowing the "current" of God to flow through the wires of our veins and nerves.

The very moment we can understand this, we have accomplished half of our journey to the experience of heaven and earth and God and man/woman. God is within us. The place where we stand is holy ground. It is up to us to activate our holiness and to activate the power that allows us to become one with God. We do this through spiritual exercises, or meditations and prayer.

Prayer and meditation are the plug that connects us to God. Prayer and meditation are invitations for God to fill us up with the divine presence, to work in us, to speak to us, and to become known to us. Prayer allows us to reach the Presence of God. Make no mistake about it. The Presence already is. The Presence always is, in sickness or in health, in lack or in abundance, in sin or in purity. The Presence of God always and already is. But it is up to us to excite, ignite, and turn on the Presence.

We ignite the Presence of God by *Practicing the Presence*. At first, the meditation won't come naturally. You will feel awkward and you will experience your mind wandering. In reality, you are training yourself to experience God. You have to do the Candle Meditation every day, again and again and again with imagination, with *kavvanah*.

I am a painter and I practice painting and sketching regularly. If you want to know Kabbalah, you have to read the text regularly. If you want to play the piano well, then you must practice every day. A beginner in learning to pray this way said to me, "But, Rabbi, this feels like so much work to pray this way." And I replied, "Anything that is worthwhile doing is work, especially at the beginning." If you want to be able to jog two miles, you begin with one lap. You make sure you exercise regularly and you try to increase your stamina as often as you can. It is the same with prayer.

We do this through perfecting our imaginative faculties and intuitive faculties through spiritual exercises. It will begin to happen soon that you will be able to focus. The separation will cease and you will feel the Presence of God. You will feel filled up with the Light of God.

Throughout the day you will continually recognize that God is within you and that the place where you stand is holy ground, that you are filled with God from head to toe. You will experience His Presence, whether it be a feeling of warmth or an intuitive feeling of His Being. But this only happens if you practice. If every morning you do the Candle Meditation that eliminates the space between you and God and if, during the day, you remember again and again that you are filled up with His light from head to toe, this is how to practice the Presence of God.

The early-twentieth-century Palestinian mystic Ha-Rav Abraham Yitzchak Kook writes in his seminal work, *Lights of Holiness:*

> The greater the person, the more he must seek to discover himself. The deep levels of his soul remain concealed from him, so he needs to be alone frequently, to elevate his imagination, to deepen his thought, to liberate his mind; finally his soul will reveal itself to him, by radiating some of His light up on him. And all will be drawn to him without hostility, jealousy and rivalry. Peace and courage will dawn on him. Compassion and love will shine on him. A zeal for accomplishment and work, a desire for action and creation, a yearning for silence and inner contemplation will join together and in his spirit he will become holy.

Liberating Concept: Healing, spirituality, and faith are available to everyone with practice

MELINDA   The universal principles are beautiful and inspiring but, like anything else worthwhile, earning the benefits takes work and we need to see/experience it in order to believe it. Faith can be acquired—more precisely, actually cognitively learned—by first practicing the spiritual exercises in this book and gaining skill, and second, seeing the results! To put it a different way, you can do these meditations and prayers regularly and see if they work for you.

When I first went to Rabbi Douglas, I was a wreck because of what was happening to my child and to myself. And here is what he did with me:

1. First he told me the stories of his healing and the healing of others. In effect, he gave me some of his faith to get me through.

2. He then taught me the Healing Prayer (given on page 59) and we did it together many times.

3. I practiced the Healing Prayer every day and it worked.

A few months later, my husband, who practices Tai Chi, gave me an article titled "A Visit to An Unique Qigong Hospital" from the magazine *Tai Chi*. The author had visited a clinic in China which was founded and run by a man who is both a *chigong* (*qigong*) grandmaster and a physician trained in both Western and Chinese medicine. (*Chigong* is the art of harnessing and using *ch'i*, the life force of the universe.)

The center avoids medicines, and instead uses a unique method of healing called *Chi Lel*. This method is based on the five-thousand-year-old concept of *chigong* as well as modern medical knowledge. According to the author, the center has had eight thousand patients and has treated more than 180 diseases with an overall success rate of more than ninety-five percent.

At this clinic, no matter how sick a person is, he or she is still addressed as "student" and never as "patient." This is because each person is learning an art, the goal of which is to heal oneself. The author also said that most of those whom he interviewed had been rejected by their former hospitals as "incurable," and the center had been their last hope.

Chi Lel consists of four parts:

1. Strong belief (*Shan Shin*). Belief that *ch'i* (life energy) can heal all ailments, including one's own. Students build belief by listening to testimonials of recovered patients and learning about ch'i and its healing effects.

Giving this kind of testimony is exactly what Rabbi Douglas did when I first walked into his office.

2. Group Healing (*Chu Chong*). Before a group of students begins *chigong*, the teacher verbally synchronizes the thinking of the group to obtain *ch'i from the universe* and bring it into a healing energy field, around everyone including him- or herself. The healing effect is enhanced because the group acts as one.

Again, this is exactly what Rabbi Douglas did with me individually and does with the group in the classes we teach.

3. *Ch'i* Healing (*Fa Ch'i*). Teachers bring healing energy from the universe to each individual to facilitate healing.

4. Practice (*Lan Gong*). Students learn easy-to-follow *chigong* movements and practice them over and over again.

I took the article to Rabbi Douglas and said: "This is spooky. It's exactly what you do and teach!"

He again smiled and replied, "Melinda, these are universal principles."

Each time Rabbi Douglas and I teach a class, a participant educates us more about the universal nature of these principles. In one recent class, for example, Geraldine Gorman introduced us to the Quaker practice of group worship. I was astonished to learn that the Quakers in their silent meetings are actually practicing the Presence of God. In the pamphlet, *The Gathered Meeting*, Thomas R. Kelly even talks about their meetings as "cases of group mysticism." It gave me goosebumps to hear Quakers speak of their own efforts to actually experience God in a language so like Rabbi Douglas's. Throughout the ages, in far distant parts of the world, healers have learned these same principles through study and experimentation. Many of them, for example, are included in the knowledge of the Christian healer Agnes Sanford. In her book, *The Healing Light*, she compares the creative energy of God to electricity that flows into an iron and makes it work. The universe is full of this creative energy, she teaches, but it has to flow through our bodies to work for us. We can learn how to pull it in and use it for healing.

This was a revolutionary Liberating Concept that freed me from thinking that God is capricious about answering prayers and that I am somehow unworthy of an answer. This liberating concept also enabled me to move into an active role, to *do* something instead of feeling powerless and helpless.

Mrs. Sanford teaches that just as we have come to understand principles that underlie electricity or light waves—things we cannot see with the naked eye—we also will come to understand the principles that underlie God's healing powers. She emphasizes that God works according to laws just as the physical universe does, and that we can learn those laws through study and practice.

Shortly after starting to work with Rabbi Douglas, I took to browsing in the meditation and religion sections of libraries and bookstores. Soon I found a remarkable series of books written by Paul Brunton, who was born in England in 1898. He pursued an interest in meditation, philosophy, and the spiritual quest through travel all over the world to learn from sages in philosophy and meditation. He then combined Western philosophy with Eastern meditation practices, discussing in many places how to meditate *to connect with and feel the presence of God.*

Again, something sounded suspiciously familiar!

Brunton wrote, "The healing powers of Nature truly exist, quite apart from the medical powers evoked by physicians, but they exist like electricity. To benefit by them we must draw them, focus them, and concentrate them on ourselves. This is done by our strong and sufficient faith, by our own concentration of attention, and by our relaxing and stilling of the whole being."

Further: "It is possible to direct the healing power of the white light, in imagination and with deep breathing, to any part of the body where pain is felt or to any organ which is not functioning properly. This does not instantly remove the trouble, but it does make a contribution towards the healing process."

Brunton offers a healing practice that involves (in summary) 1) relaxation with a focus on breathing that draws in the "curative force from Nature"; 2) calling upon "the One Infinite Life-Power, filling all space and pervading the entire universe, existing everywhere, containing and permeating all creatures, all humanity, including one's self"; and 3) concentrating this Power by placing the hands on the affected part of the body.

Rabbi Douglas teaches that there are no supernatural miracles because healing happens through the natural process. Agnes Sanford and Paul Brunton taught the same principle. In Brunton's words: "There are no miracles in Nature, but there are happenings to which science possesses no key. . . . powers and phenomena may seem miraculous, but they really issue forth from the hidden laws of man's own being. The processes take place in the dark only to us."

Rabbi Douglas and I have taught a series of "Healing Meditations" in the past four years. In a recent class, a participant knowledgeable about Reiki shared more evidence of these universal principles.

The "Rei" part of Reiki, I learned, means "universal." A more sophisticated meaning is "spiritual consciousness," or "wisdom that comes from God or the Higher Self." The "Ki" part of Reiki is identified as the Life Force which is the same as the Chinese *ch'i*. It is called the life force or the vital life force or the universal life force. So a more complete definition of Reiki is: spiritually guided life force or energy.

And, just as Rabbi Douglas often reminds us that one must be a good person for the prayer he teaches to work, so in Reiki it is necessary to live and act in a way that promotes harmony with others.

The material reviewed here is only a fraction of what a scholar could find. My examples were discovered through casual browsing and, even then, the similarities were astonishing. The key is: I can learn to have faith, and I can find God through Practicing Her/His Presence.

Whenever I find myself doubting or falling into uncertainty and fear (not keeping the presence of God with me), I begin to do a *mantra* meditation on a verse from the Book of Proverbs that increases my trust in God. The results are amazing. The next "How To" section is about this meditation.

How to Do It

MEDITATION ON PROVERBS 3:5

RABBI
DOUGLAS
In my experience, *mantra* meditation is very helpful. The ancient rabbis often focused on a word or a Biblical verse. I have found that when I use a Biblical verse that I have faith in, I receive a transcendental state of attachment to the Divine. This was a common practice of many of the Jewish mystics.

A favorite Biblical verse of mine is found in Proverbs 3:5. I translate it as: "Trust in the Lord with all your might. Do not depend on your own understanding. Acknowledge Him in all your ways; then He will direct your paths." This verse maintains that if one trusts in God, there is no fear. Keep in mind that the Hebrew word *binah*, which is commonly translated as "understanding," is more aptly translated as "worry" in this verse. So this Proverb means: "Do not depend (focus) on your own worry."

I have seen in moments of despair that when I put my complete trust in the Lord, God comes through. Furthermore, when I meditate on this text, knowing with faith that God will come through, I am joyous and happy. I suggest meditating on this Biblical verse, reading it, repeating it, and reciting it as a *mantra*. This will bring you into a state of joy.

1. Find a comfortable and restful place in which you are not likely to be disturbed. Make yourself comfortable, loosening any tight fitting clothing.

2. Recite "Trust in the Lord with all your might. Do not depend on your own understanding. Acknowledge Him in all your ways; then He will direct your paths" for several minutes until you feel a state of elevated ecstasy. You will feel joyous, knowing that God is with you.

5: HEALING PRAYER

Universal Principle: Healing Prayer is for everyone

RABBI DOUGLAS   I WAS nervous when I met Rabbi Dresher for the first time. I was a Reform rabbi and he was a Hasidic rabbi. Would he chastise me for not observing all the commandments? Reform Jewish people use the Torah as a guide, whereas Hasidic and Orthodox Jews understand the Torah and all its commandments to be God's revealed word that one must strive to observe and put into practice.

As a Reform Jew, I observe some commandments literally and others metaphorically. An Orthodox Jew must observe all the commandments literally. I felt that Rabbi Dresher would not see me as a sincere religious leader, and that he would demean Reform Judaism. I also felt that once he saw that I am non-Orthodox, he would not want to pray with me. I had visions of losing my leg and not being able to walk because I am a Reform Jew.

I was so nervous that I asked my wife Peggy to come with me and meet the rabbi. We rang the bell. Rabbi Dresher himself opened the door. My first words were: "My wife came with me."

He replied, "Good. You need her."

We entered his apartment.

Now, I love books and I have many books. My synagogue study is filled with thousands of them. But his living room looked like a public library, with Hebrew books from floor to ceiling, and books of all shapes and sizes on his desk and chairs. I counted two different sets of the Talmud and several Hebrew Bibles.

We sat down. We told him about my disease and he said, "Good.

We will pray together." He began by telling me that I would need to pray with someone on a regular basis—someone who loves me and respects me and is willing to pray with and for me every day. I knew this would be my wife. I remember asking him, "Why do I need another person to pray with and for me? Why can't I do the prayer myself?"

He said, "Do you have pain?"

I answered, "I have lots of pain."

"Can you walk without your cane?"

"I can't walk without my cane."

"You need a prayer partner." And he took down a volume of Talmud, Tractate *Berachos*. We turned to page 5b and he read:

> Rabbi Chiya bar Abba was ill. Rabbi Yochanan went to visit him and he asked him, "Are your sufferings dear to you?" Rabbi Chiya bar Abba answered him, "Neither they nor their reward." Rabbi Yochanan said to him, "Give me your hand." Rabbi Chiya bar Abba gave him his hand and Rabbi Yochanan revived him.
>
> A similar incident took place when Rabbi Yochanan was ill. Rabbi Chanina went to visit him, and asked him, "Are these sufferings dear to you?" Rabbi Yochanan answered him, "Neither they nor their reward." Rabbi Chanina said to him, "Give me your hand." Rabbi Yochanan gave him his hand and Rabbi Chanina revived him.

Then, the Talmud asks, "Why did Rabbi Yochanan need Rabbi Chanina's help? Can't Rabbi Yochanan pray for himself ? The Talmud answers that "a captive cannot release himself from prison." This teaches that a person who is ill and has pain and is suffering needs someone to pray for him or her. The person needs outside help.

Rabbi Dresher made it clear to me that because my illness was my prison, I needed a prayer partner to lift me from my prison.

After the rabbi showed me how important it is to have a prayer partner, he then shared with me the great healing text of the Hebrew Scriptures—the passage that elucidates how Moses healed his sister Miriam from her awful disease of leprosy.

When they were in Hazeroth, Miriam and Aaron spoke against Moses because of the Cushite woman he had married: "He married a Cushite woman!"

They said, "Has the Lord spoken only through Moses? Has He not spoken through us as well." The Lord heard it. Now Moses was a very humble man more so than any other man on earth. Suddenly the Lord called to Moses, Aaron, and Miriam, "Come out, you three, to the Tent of Meeting." So the three of them went out. The Lord came down in a pillar of cloud, stopped at the entrance of the Tent, and called out, "Aaron and Miriam?" The two of them came forward; and He said, "Hear these My words: When a prophet of the Lord arises among you, I make Myself known to him in a vision, I speak with him in a dream. Not so with My servant Moses; he is trusted throughout My household. With him I speak mouth to mouth, plainly and not in riddles, and he beholds the likeness of the Lord. How then did you not shrink from speaking against My servant Moses!" Still incensed with them, the Lord departed.

As the cloud withdrew from the Tent, there was Miriam stricken with snow-white scales! When Aaron turned toward Miriam, he saw that she was stricken with scales. And Aaron said to Moses, "O my Lord, account not to us the sin which we committed in our folly. Let her not be as one dead, who emerges from his mother's womb with half his flesh eaten away." So Moses cried out to the Lord, saying, "O God, pray heal her."

But the Lord said to Moses, "If her father spat in her face, would she not bear her shame for seven days? Let her be shut out of camp for seven days, and then let her be readmitted." So Miriam was shut out of camp seven days; and the people did not march on until Miriam was readmitted. After that the people set out from Hazeroth and encamped in the wilderness of Paran. (Numbers 12:1–16)

When Moses marries Zipporah, an Ethiopian (Cushite) woman, who is black and non-Israelite, Miriam and Aaron are disturbed. They criticize Moses for abandoning his own community and reaching out for a wife from another community. It is clear that they are angry at Moses because they feel he arbitrarily withdrew from their community and reached out into another community. Furthermore, this new wife is black.

When Miriam protests, she and Aaron challenge Moses' unique claim to prophecy. "They said, 'Has the Lord spoken only through Moses? Has He not spoken through us as well?' The Lord heard it." (Numbers 12:2) Also, it is clear that they challenged Moses' decision to marry outside their race, because Miriam's punishment was that she became leprous, as "white as snow." In other words, her desire for her brother to marry a white woman was ironically shown by the text since she herself became very, very white—a symptom of leprosy. When she becomes ill, she recognizes her mistake, and Aaron invites Moses to heal her. Then Moses prays a prayer that is among the most powerful healing prayers in all scripture, "O God, pray heal Miriam now."

Rabbi Dresher taught me that this simple healing verse was the basis for his healing prayer, which was derived from Scriptural and Kabbalistic sources. I used this prayer to help me during my time of extreme illness. I used this prayer when my wife had cancer, and when Melinda was ill. I've also used this prayer with many other members of my synagogue community with excellent results. At the end of this chapter, we describe how to do this special healing prayer.

While Rabbi Dresher was teaching me healing prayer, he emphasized how important it was for myself and the person praying for me to understand that not only am I created in the image of God, but if I want the prayer to succeed, I must realize that I am filled with the Presence of God. And the vision that I have of the Presence of God should be a vision of light, filling me from head to toe, filling my chest cavity, my arms, my fingers, my legs, my toes. This vision, in part, comes about through the Candle Meditation which was influenced by the *Zohar* (p. 14). But now, I must do more to fill myself with the Presence of God. I must recognize the God within and without me, for God is indeed everywhere. After I have embraced and become one with God through the Candle Meditation, I must also embrace God even more and bring down God's light from above, basking in God's sunlight.

Rabbi Dresher taught me that I should stretch forth my arms to the heavens when I pray for healing, with my palms facing upwards, imagining two columns of bright light coming down from the heavens into the palms of my hands. He taught me to concentrate with *kavvanah* on the two columns of light, feeling the warmth of the light in the palms of my hands. And as I feel the warm light, I should recognize and know that I am making contact with the Divine Presence.

This is what Rabbi Dresher told me as he reached for a copy of the *Zohar,* turning to the commentary on Exodus, where it says of verse 7:11: "And come and see, when a man raises his hand in prayer, he directs his fingers toward the heavens as it is written, it came to pass that when Moses raised his hand, Israel prevailed." The *Zohar* teaches that when one raises his hands with the ten fingers outstretched, these ten fingers symbolize the unification of the ten *Sefirot.* (The ten *Sefirot* in Jewish mysticism symbolize the unity of God. For an explanation of the *Sefirot,* see pages 105–113) Rabbi Dresher emphasized how important it is to reach out with one's hands to receive the Presence of God. Then he told me to concentrate with *kavvanah* on bringing down God's illuminating light into the palms of my hand. He told me to visualize these rays of light with deep concentration, for the *Zohar* text says, "And then he concentrates on bringing blessing down from above."

Then Rabbi Dresher showed us how to pour the light on one another. Peggy, my wife, poured the light on my left leg, filling it with light and continually imagining that she was a vehicle of God's power. She continually prayed with *kavvanah.* And as she poured the light of God on me, she recited five times, "El Na Rifa Na La"—the same prayer that Moses prayed for his sister Miriam.

Rabbi Dresher told Peggy and me to visualize myself healed, to see me walking briskly without a cane. He told us that the great healing rabbi, the Ba'al Shem Tov, taught that when one prays for healing, one visualizes being already healed, because a prayer that is brought forth before God has already been answered. Rabbi Dresher taught me that this is the way that one prays with faith.

Then we conclude our prayer in the spirit of the Ba'al Shem Tov, thanking God for having healed us—not thanking God for healing us tomorrow, not thanking God for healing us next week, but recognizing that God's healing *has already begun.* With our mind's eye, we see ourselves healed.

Liberating Concept: I can do this!

MELINDA   This Healing Prayer works. In the last five years, I have seen and experienced many, many successes. My aunt, Sr. Cecile Marie, a Franciscan nun, recently wrote to me: "Melinda, your prayer group must be powerful pray-ers. They certainly brought me back to new life. Please thank them again for me. I am feeling fine. Just have to get sufficient rest. Can hardly believe I am eighty-two years old *but I am!* However, I really feel young in spirit!" She continued, "The other sisters and I are patiently waiting for your precious book. We will be very happy and proud to get it into many hands. This is exactly where our community is going."

My faith began to build five years ago with my own bodily healing. I suffered from ovarian cysts for more than a year. Such cysts are only life-threatening in a small percentage of cases, but they were painful enough to wake me up at night.

I had tried many different things—including surgery, medication, Chinese herbs, and vitamins prescribed by an acupuncturist—without success. My family uses any and all types of healers. My son's headaches were healed by a neurologist, my husband's shoulder by a Chinese acupuncturist, my bad knee by an orthopedist, etc. But nothing had worked for my cysts until I tried this Healing Prayer. The Healing Prayer took away the cysts.

I know this is true and not just coincidence or the power of suggestion because at first I truly thought I was doing the prayer right, but the pain persisted. After a couple of weeks, I went back to see Rabbi Douglas. I was discouraged and depressed—chronic pain does that. He asked me to describe exactly how I was praying and then he said: "Oops, I forgot to tell you this important part." And, when I added that part, the pain started to go away. It took a few more weeks of regularly saying the prayer for the pain to be completely gone. I also know that it is the prayer that healed the cysts because for the first year if I missed a day or two of prayers, the pain started to come back!!!

If you have ever suffered chronic pain or watched a child suffer, you know that there is no mistaking having pain and not having pain. You know the difference! This really works!

I suggested that Rabbi Douglas find a way to share this with more people. As a psychotherapist, I work to alleviate suffering. It is my life mission. The results of the meditations and prayer were so stunning. I just didn't want anyone on earth to have to suffer what my child or I went through.

Rabbi Douglas asked me to write this book with him. This was very flattering and gratifying. However, the knowledge that is taught here is the result of twenty-seven years of study and work by Rabbi Douglas. He is one of those people whom I call the "truly gifted." I struggled for a couple of weeks with "What do I have to offer here?" I am not "truly gifted." Only a short time before I had been a tremendous doubter and was a "big zero" in the spirituality, healing, and meditation department. Then it came to me. What I have to offer here is that I am ordinary and these teachings still worked for me. My life is hectic with two children, a husband, a career, and a house to run. I have read about people who embrace meditation. Often they write things like: Well, I just decided that every day I would get up at 5 A.M. to meditate. That is not me.

Most of the time I've done these meditations hiding out in the bathroom from a house full of children with the lights out and a candle lit and a child knocking on the door asking something like, "Where are my shoes?" or "Are you almost done?" I don't have the lifestyle; I don't have the concentration; I don't have the discipline. My role in this book is to share with you that this can work for anyone with persistence. If I can do this, anyone can do this.

In the classes that Rabbi Douglas and I have taught, people would come up to me and ask with awe, "Can you pray like the Rabbi?" or "Do you have the perfect faith that he is talking about?" And, I would answer honestly, "Oh, no, not even close!" In analyzing my success, I deduced that the reason the prayer worked for me was that I had a wonderful prayer partner, my husband, Jim. The key was praying with great love and persistence even when we were beginners and could barely concentrate. The Greater Mind, praying with the perfect faith that the healing has already begun and will be successful, only comes with practice.

One reason that having a prayer partner is crucial is that prayer in a group is more powerful. Another reason is that even though I have had success praying for short periods for myself alone, it is impossible to sustain joy and faith when one is sick. It is inevitable that illness and pain cause depression and fear. When one cannot fully experience faith and joy, your prayer partner comes through.

Again, if you pray with great love and persistence, the Healing Prayer will be successful for you. I cannot emphasize enough: *If I can do this, anyone can!*

How to Do It

HEALING PRAYER

RABBI
DOUGLAS
1. Do the Candle Meditation, and feel as though you are completely filled with God's light. You and the light of God are one.

2. Begin to say repeatedly with eyes closed and with mounting energy the following meditative prayer derived from Psalms 27:1 and 30:2:

> The Lord is my strength
>
> The Lord is my life
>
> The Lord is my light
>
> The Lord is my healing.

3. As you repeatedly say this out loud, you will begin to feel a mounting energy. The room will feel full of God's healing energy. At this point, you stand and turn your palms up at about eye level with your fingers facing away from you. Try to feel two columns of light coming down from the heavens into the palm of each hand. Concentrate and visualize the light. Remember prayer is an art, and this visualization takes practice. With practice and experience and time, you will feel the heat. When you see the light and feel the heat, turn your palms to face the person that needs healing. Pour

this light on that person's heart or lungs or nose—any part of the body that needs healing.

4. Concentrate on your love for God, God's love for you, and the love you have for who you are praying for. You cannot hold resentment for who you are praying for. Nor can they hold resentment for you.

5. Continue to feel the light in your palms shining on the other person and say five times Moses' healing prayers in Hebrew. The Hebrew letters and words have mystical powers.

    El Na Rifa Na La   El Na Rifa Na La

    El Na Rifa Na La   El Na Rifa Na La

    El Na Rifa Na La

Oh God, heal _____ now. (Put the ill person's name in the space.)

You say this healing prayer with faith and belief that it is working now. Belief is of utmost importance. Without belief, without faith, without the Heightened Consciousness, prayer has little chance of working.

In English, the words *El Na Rifa Na La* mean, "O God, heal _____ now."

6. As you continue to pour God's light on the person, say personal prayers. As you pray, concentrate on how much you love the person you are praying for.

7. See the person you are praying for, completely healed, doing some activity that he or she can only do when well. Know that the person is healed and you say, "Oh give thanks to the Lord for He is Good, for His healing continues every day." And say with perfect faith, as you know the healing has taken place, "Thank you God for having healed _____."

You can do this healing prayer for yourself as well. It does not have to be done only for another person, but it is important that you work with a prayer partner.

6: THE COMMANDMENT TO REJOICE

Universal Principle: Joy brings healing

RABBI DOUGLAS MANY YEARS AGO, there was a farmer named Moshe who made his home in the Ukraine in the nineteenth century. Those who knew Moshe called him "Moshe Simcha," joyous Moshe. He always had a big smile on his face. It's not that his life was full of joyful experiences, but he recognized that it's easier to smile than to frown. It happened that Moshe was farming his land one day, when his plow hit a large, strange-looking stone. He picked up the stone and thought to himself, "This must be valuable. It shines like a rare diamond."

Moshe brought the stone to his brother-in-law Shabbtai, a jeweler. When Shabbtai saw the huge, unusual stone, he immediately asked Moshe where he found this rare gem. Moshe answered, "It must have fallen from the heavens."

Then, Moshe asked Shabbtai, "How much do you think this is worth?"

Shabbtai responded, "I am not sure, but it must be worth a lot of money. You will have to take it to Amsterdam. Jewelers there will be able to pay the price for such a large stone."

Moshe thought to himself, "How will I get to Amsterdam? I can't afford the boat ride to Holland. I'm only a poor farmer." He asked Shabbtai to help with the arrangements. So, his brother-in-law contacted a sly and shady captain he knew, a smuggler by trade, who had a ship going to Amsterdam in a few days.

"I'll take you to Amsterdam, but I want to be paid by cash when we arrive," the captain said. Moshe thought to himself, "I will have money when I sell the diamond, so I will be able to pay my fare then." So, he agreed and was given a private cabin.

The captain was an ugly, bearded man whose mouth twitched and who had a hook for a hand. As a matter of fact, each day, he would boast to Moshe of the men he had killed because they had tried to cheat him. Most people would be terrified of this evil man, but Moshe, with his joyous soul, always saw things in a joyous perspective. Every time he saw the captain's mouth twitch, he thought of his ugly sister-in-law, which made him laugh. And every time the captain boasted of the men he had murdered, Moshe thought of Haman, the Jew-hater, and he pictured the captain hanging at the gallows as did Haman.

And so, every time Moshe saw the captain, he laughed. The captain thought he was laughing at his jokes, so they got along fine during the long sea journey.

Every day after he finished lunch, Moshe took the stone out of the dirty handkerchief, in which he kept it, and he would gaze at his stone. Under a rough, dirty exterior, the stone shone so brilliantly, it was as if there were stars embedded in the stone. The more he looked at the stone, the more he came to love it. He regretted that he would soon have to sell it.

One day, as Moshe was examining his stone, mesmerized by its beauty, he fell asleep, leaving the stone on the dining table, loosely wrapped in the handkerchief. The steward, thinking the stone was an ordinary rock, threw it overboard with the other garbage from the table.

When Moshe woke up, he immediately realized his stone was gone, lost forever. He had no money to pay for his passage on the boat. He was terrified. "If I tell the captain the truth about the stone, I'm a dead man. I will have to make the best of this situation." So, what did he do? He continued to put a smile on his face and joked with the captain, just like in previous days. The captain had no idea of Moshe's troubles.

The day before they were to arrive in Amsterdam, the captain approached Moshe and said, "People don't know me in Holland. I wonder if we could have the entire cargo put in your name. The customs officer will think you are a rich businessman. They won't bother you. I'm afraid they will give me a hard time. I will pay you handsomely for this favor."

What could Moshe do? If he said, "No," he would be thrown overboard. If he said "Yes" and the customs officials realized the shipment was smuggled goods, he would only go to jail. So, of course, he agreed. Moshe signed the papers and immediately, on paper, he was a wealthy man.

There was a storm that night. The storm was so rough and the winds were so wicked, that several of the sailors were blown overboard. Including the captain.

Moshe was now a very wealthy man. He gave all the sailors a big bonus, and was still very rich. When Moshe returned home, his neighbors saw that he was even more joyful than before. Furthermore, he had a new habit of giving away money. And people began to smile just as Moshe always smiled.

Whenever my grandfather told me this story of Moshe Simcha, he would smile . . . and so would I.

Told by Rabbi Nachman of Bratslav

Last October, during the Jewish High Holy Days, I delivered a sermon to my congregation on the importance of being happy. I stressed that not only is it fun to be happy, not only is it healthy to be happy, but, more importantly, as Jewish people we are *commanded* to be happy.

Our Torah has 613 commandments (*mitzvot*) within it. One of these commandments is found in the Book of Deuteronomy, the fifth book of our Torah. At that time, the Jews are given instruction by Moses in God's law. And Moses begins his legal lecture by saying, "These are the laws and rules which you must carefully observe in the land that the Lord, God of your fathers, is giving you to possess, as long as you live on earth." (Deuteronomy 12:1) And then in the midst of these statutes, Moses articulates God's command, "And you shall rejoice before the Lord your God with your sons and daughters . . ." (Deuteronomy 12:12) A few verses later, Moses emphasizes this statute of God when he says *"vi-Hayita ach same'ach,"* which means "You are commanded to rejoice." (Deuteronomy 16:15)

After I shared this scriptural insight in my sermon on Rosh Hashanah, many of my parishioners approached me and commented on how meaningful this text was for them. They were unaware that God not only suggests happiness, but commands happiness.

Being joyous is part of our tradition. Rejoicing is essential to the Jewish faith.

Purim, for example, is a holiday celebrating the victory of the Jewish people, under the leadership of Mordecai, over the anti-Semitic Haman and his followers. The story is found in the Book of Esther, which teaches that when the Jews were exiled in Persia, they prospered until Prime Minister Haman, under the rule of King Ahasuerus, wanted to exterminate the Jews of Persia. His plan was foiled by the king's wife, a Jewess named Esther, and her scholarly uncle Mordecai.

Haman picked lots to decide when he would do away with the Jews. The Hebrew word for "lots" is *pur,* and the holiday remembering the victory of the Jews is called Purim. It is held in late winter around the world in the Hebrew month of Adar. Traditionally at Purim, Jews are commanded to get so drunk that we cannot distinguish between the evil Haman and the good Mordecai!

Oh, it's easy and simple to rejoice when you're happy. But God doesn't say, "You shall only rejoice when you're happy." The Torah says, "You are commanded to rejoice"—whether you're happy or whether you're sad, whether you are rich or poor.

Sure, it's easy to rejoice when things are going well—you just won the lottery, you just got a big raise at work, you just started your vacation. But God doesn't ask you to praise Him only when things go well. We are to also worship God joyfully when things are not running smoothly in our lives. The High Holy Day Union Prayer Book begins its day-long prayers for Rosh Hashanah with the exclamation, "As we thank Thee for the joys of life, so we praise Thee for its sorrows."

And yet, I recognize, as do most of my parishioners, that the commandment to rejoice is not always easy.

Two years ago, when my wife was recuperating from cancer, I was asked to officiate at the wedding of a member of our synagogue. Peggy had just come home from the hospital that week, and she was in great pain. Our prayers had worked. She was cancer-free, but she was not comfortable and she was still very weak. But I had to leave her and go officiate at the wedding.

The food was wonderful. The drinks were plentiful. The music was excellent. People were dancing and singing and clapping. It appeared everyone was happy but me. Everyone was rejoicing but me. That night I couldn't sing. I couldn't dance because that evening I kept thinking about Peggy and her pain and her cancer operation. I couldn't be happy.

I knew it is a *mitzvah* to rejoice, but then I only knew it intellectually. I didn't really practice the *mitzvah* that night. I had a sad face. I had a sad soul.

It was only later that I realized that since God has given us the ability to rejoice, God wants us to rejoice. And there is a reason for this commandment. When I am in a wedding and I am acting sad, when I am worrying because I think that Peggy's recovery is not going well, this means I lack faith in God. This means I don't trust in God's healing power. That's why God gave us the command, "*vi-Hayita ach same'ach* . . . You are commanded to rejoice."

It's another way of saying, "Have faith in me." God tells us, "I know your wife is sick, but enjoy the wedding. Have faith in me. Trust me. I will make things work out. Your wife will be well." That's why Scripture says, "Trust in the Lord with all your might. Do not depend on your own understanding. Acknowledge Him in all your ways; then He will direct your paths." (Proverbs 3:5) So, when God says, "You are commanded to rejoice," God means "Don't be sad. Don't lose faith. Don't give up hope. Rejoice, for *I am here.*"

The commandment to rejoice also means to bring joy to other people. We have to bring happiness to other people. It is not enough to experience happiness. Sometimes we feel sad, sometimes we feel depressed. But we still have to bring joy to others. It's hard to do.

When I was at that wedding, my responsibility was to bring joy to the room, joy to the bride and groom, joy to the people, and not make myself feel sad. I learned. When Peggy and I go to weddings now, we always go on the dance floor. I always do the jitterbug. It reminds me of my good old days in high school—

I went to Outremont High School in Montreal, Quebec. During the lunch hour every Friday, we used to have school dance contests. We had one and a half hours for lunch—ten minutes for eating, an hour and twenty minutes for dancing. I won many dance contests. At that time, it was easier for me to rejoice on the dance floor than it is today at age fifty-four, when my bones ache when I have to do more than two jitterbugs in a row!

For twenty-seven years now, I have led services in sign language and voice for our synagogue of deaf and hearing people. We have a wonderful choir with a soloist who chants the melodies while the rest of the choir signs the liturgy in American Sign Language.

In every Jewish house of worship on the Sabbath, you will see boys, girls, men, and even women in many synagogues, march with the many Torahs around the sanctuary. This custom, called *Hakafot*, inspires great joy since the Jews are given the opportunity to kiss the Torah, remembering that the Torah again is the marriage contract between God and Israel on this special Sabbath wedding day. For many years, during our Sabbath services, when we removed the Torah from the Ark, I used to dance in front of the Ark with Edith, a deaf blind lady. As the Torah procession continued, and as the choir signed the melodies with their elegant and graceful hands, and as the soloist sang the ancient Hebrew liturgy, Edith and I would dance ecstatically. She could not hear the music or see me, but when she danced, her joy was so great that it was intoxicating. It was as if we all became drunk with joy at this unique dance.

Dancing with Edith on Shabbat always reminded me of a wonderful story that Martin Buber relates about expressing joy through dancing:

News was brought to Rabbi Moishe Leib that his friend, the Rabbi of Berditchev had fallen ill. On the Sabbath, he said his

name over and over and prayed for his recovery. Then he put on
new shoes made of Moroccan leather, laced them up tight and
danced.

A Tzaddik (an extraordinarily good person) who was present,
said, "Power flowed forth from his dancing. Every step was a
powerful mystery. And unfamiliar light suffused the house and
everyone watching saw the heavenly host join in his dance."

When Edith and I danced, our joy was so great that we forgot our
troubles and our pains. This dance of joy propelled us, and the congregation, into a higher state of consciousness. This ecstatic joy brought
us all closer to God.

In the early years of our synagogue, there was an elderly deaf man
who regularly came to the Sabbath service. He always carried the
Torah with pride. I have fond memories of his beautiful and eloquent
signs as he prayed the prayers.

After services, I would usually drive him home. He lived far from
our temple in an area of Chicago called Logan Square. Now, I don't
know why, but every Friday night as I was driving him home, the gas
gauge of the car read "empty." I always pointed this out to Richard,
and would make facial expressions to tease him. I knew it wasn't nice
to tease an eighty-two-year-old man, but it was part of our Sabbath
ritual, and he enjoyed teasing me back. More importantly, we always
arrived at his home safely. I had faith that we would, and we always
did, even though the gas gauge was almost always empty. Of course,
I also knew that even though the gas gauge registered empty, you could
still drive several more miles on the reserve gasoline in the car!

I think what God means by, "You are commanded to rejoice" is
this: "When you feel tired, when you feel worn out, when you feel you
can't go on any more—rejoice! There is a reserve of gasoline left inside
of you." There is inside each person the capacity to do more than we
think we can do. And this capacity inside us—that's from God. And
that's why, if we rejoice even though times are hard, we will inspire
the God within us, and we will become strong.

We Jews look forward to our Sabbath, our Shabbat, because it is
a time of joy for all of us. We see it as a Bride, and we celebrate it

like a wedding. We welcome it with a special hymn, *"L'Cha Dodi,"* uttering the words, "Welcome, Sabbath the Bride, Queen of our Days." Many Jewish congregations stand up and face the door as they sing *"L'Cha Dodi,"* welcoming the Sabbath bride every Friday night. This prayer reminds us that the Sabbath is a time of great joy. "They who keep the Sabbath and call it a delight rejoice in Thy kingdom. All who hallow the Sabbath day shall be gladdened by Thy goodness. This day is Israel's festival of the spirit, sanctified and blessed by Thee, the most precious of days, a symbol of the joy of Creation."

After services, we have a festive dessert in the synagogue. It's called the *Oneg Shabbat,* which means "Sabbath Delight." When I was a boy in Montreal, we used to have Turkish delights as part of our *Oneg Shabbat* after the Shabbat meal in our home.

Our tradition also asks us, even today, to dress in our finest garments on Shabbat. Just as a groom is dressed in his finest clothes, so are we to dress in our finest clothes on the Sabbath, as it is the wedding day between Israel and her God. It is also a wedding day on which Israel and her Sabbath bride are united by God. On this wedding day, there is a mysticism that transcends an ordinary wedding day. For the Jews believe that on the eve of the Sabbath, the Lord gives each person a *Neshamah Yeterah,* an additional soul. With this soul, we dance with joy as we receive the Torah once again from Sinai.

There are those who argue that this *Neshamah Yeterah* is figurative. To me, it seems quite real. When we enter our synagogue on Friday night or Saturday morning, and see the signing and hear the clapping, and watch the dancing, we know that there is something especially joyous here. You can feel the healing. You can see a direct correlation between joy and healing.

Jewish tradition maintains that there is a direct correlation between joy and healing. This is because joy is a prerequisite for the manifestation of the Holy Spirit, and there is no healing without God's Holy Spirit. The Jewish mystic Chaim Vital[1] wrote in the introduction to *Sha'ar Ha-Kavvanot* that when one prays, one should not pray in sadness or with a contrite heart unless one is praying the Yom Kippur prayers. In regular prayer, one should pray with exceptional joy, just like a servant who serves his master with great joy and happiness.

When we pray with exceptional joy, we are able to bring down the Divine Light from above. It is as if a joyous body and soul form a conduit for the Spirit of God. Indeed, we learn that King David danced with joy before the Ark of the Lord. "And David and all the house of Yisrae'el played before the Lord on all manner of instruments made of cypress wood, on lyres, and on lutes, and on timbrels . . . And David leaped about before the Lord with all his might. . . . So David and all the house of Israel brought up the Ark of the Lord with shouting, and with the sound of the shofar." (II Samuel 6:5, 14–15)

The Bible teaches that when we pray, we should pray with all our bones and sinews, (Psalm 35:10) for this releases the endorphins of joy that are stored up within us. We do this regularly every Sabbath at our synagogue. We not only utter the praises of God with our mouth, but we sign with our hands, releasing great joy just as the Psalmist commands.

According to Martin Buber, Rabbi Nachman of Bratslav (1772–1810) was the last great Jewish mystic. He was also the great grandson of the revered Ba'al Shem Tov. Rabbi Nachman maintains, in his magnum opus *Likutey Moharan: The Collected Teaching of Rabbi Nachman of Bratslav,* that inherent in rejoicing are powerful healing forces. He underlines the Biblical injunction to rejoice by stating, ". . . *mitzvah gedolah lihyot bisimcha tamid*"—"It is a great *mitzvah* to be always happy."

In this teaching, the Kabbalistic Rabbi Nachman teaches that joy or *simcha*, leads to healing:

It is a great *mitzvah* to be happy all the time, and to use strength, and with strength, you escape from sadness and depression. All the illnesses that come to an individual come because of lack of joy. . . . The main principle is that one must muster all his strength into rejoicing at all times. It is man's nature to let himself become depressed and sad. On account of the difficulties in life, each person has a life of suffering. Because of this, all man has an obligation to rejoice continually and to be happy in whatever way he can. Even with different kinds of humor. It is true that a contrite heart is good. But only for a short time. It is appropriate to set aside a certain time every day to examine oneself and make contrition before God. But then, throughout the day, one should be happy and rejoice, because a contrite heart which leads to depression is much worse than a joyous heart which leads to frivolity. Contrition is more likely to lead to melancholy. Therefore, one should always rejoice and be happy—only at set times should one experience a contrite heart.

Rabbi Nachman was a leading figure of the Hasidic Jewish movement, a unique populist Jewish movement which began in Poland-Lithuania in the eighteenth century. Literally, the word "Hasidim" means "the pious ones." These Hasidim developed a system of prayers and teachings based on the work of the Kabbalistic genius Isaac Luria.[2]

Their teachings were populist in that they maintained that every individual has a right to be joyous, and that prayer and study should be joyous activities. They danced and sang during their religious services. This was very different than the other Jewish communities at that time, who worshipped and studied with meticulous attention to *halakhic* details and strict observance of the law. (*Halakha* is that aspect of Jewish literature which deals with the Jewish legal tradition. The Hebrew word *Halakha* usually refers to Talmudic law and the great bodies of Jewish law, such as the *Shulkhan Aruch*.) This is not to say that the Hasidim disregarded the law. On the contrary, they vigorously maintained *halakha*, but they did this in a free-flowing joyful manner.

Hasidic fervor in the belief that all things that happen are for the good and Hasidic joy (*simcha*) are based on the idea that everything is in God. Since everything is within the Belly of God, this includes man's sorrows—but since man's sorrows are in the Belly of God and do not have independent existence, there is no reason for despair. When people rejoice, especially when they rejoice because they know they are an instrument of God, they inspire divine joy from above and blessings flow throughout their life and throughout all creation. This is a spiritual law of gravity. Just as the physical law maintains that what goes up must come down, the spiritual law maintains that joy on earth inspires joy in the heavens, which necessarily brings down God's blessings.

A mood of depression is anathema to Hasidism; this separates man from his God. A person should not grieve much, even over his or her sins, because only in joy can we reach God, not in sorrow.

The basic idea of joy in Hasidism is illustrated in this Hasidic tale about the legendary early charismatic Hasidic leader, Israel b. Eliezer Ba'al Shem Tov. The Besht, as he was called, was not only a rabbi knowledgeable in Torah. He was also a popular healer who participated in ecstatic prayer and influenced thousands of followers.

> Several Hasidim came to the Besht and said, "Our opponents, the Sages of Brody, persecute us continually and accuse us, heaven forbid, of disobedience to the Law and irreverence toward the traditions of our forefathers. We can endure it no longer, and we must answer them."
>
> "Our adversaries," replied the Besht, "do this certainly out of pious zeal. They believe they are performing a good deed, and they take joy in oppressing us. Why should we seek to deprive them of their joy?"

Liberating Concept: Joy takes work, too!

MELINDA   Rabbi Douglas's sermon on Rosh Hashanah hit me like a bolt of lightning. In my years of struggling to understand emotional healing, I had searched for a key and here it was: JOY. My husband, Jim, got it, too. When the sermon was finished, he leaned over and whispered with no small amount of humor, "How often does someone get a sermon written just for them?" It was very funny but also very revealing. I am a world-class worrier. The Commandment to Rejoice was another Liberating Concept for me!

My education in emotional healing began many years ago, first as a special education teacher, and then as a graduate student at the University of Chicago. The greatest part of my learning about psychotherapy came from Heinz Kohut, the founder of Self Psychology, a school of psychoanalytic theory and practice. He wrote that "the capacity to enjoy life . . . . is an indicator of successful living. . . ."

That just about sums it up, but what a task for us humans! How does one get out of worry and into joy? The human psyche is often as much a mystery as the world of subatomic particles or the vast universe. Just as frequently as there is a new discovery in physics that changes how we view the physical world, there is a discovery in the field of mental health that changes how we view our brains and emotions.

Research has shown that our emotions are the result of a complicated intertwining of experience and biology. Feelings of depression and anxiety can come from childhood experiences, as the result of trauma in adulthood, and/or from an inherited vulnerability to a neurobiological disorder. For example, the magazine *Psychology Today* recently published a review of research on depression. Depression is no longer thought to be purely a disorder of neurotransmitters but rather a disruption of a neural circuit that runs among several brain structures. This faulty circuitry can be seen with highly sophisticated brain imaging techniques. There are many interrelated results including one part of the brain initiating an intense, prolonged reaction to stress. Other parts of the brain fail to generate positive feelings and inhibit disruptive negative ones.

These discoveries confirm my professional and personal experience that the best treatments combine interactive work such as psychotherapy and self-help groups along with the physiological. Since we are social creatures, trauma and faulty brain function impact both how we experience ourselves and how others experience us—the building blocks of self-concept and relationships. Physiological help can include medication, exercise, intensive relearning techniques, meditation, and more.

Certain fundamentals are necessary for the experience of joy. In Heinz Kohut's beautiful words, we require a self that has cohesion, strength, and harmony. We need to feel alive, real and worthwhile. We must evoke the "empathic resonance" of healthy people and be "sustained" by them.

Just as with physical healing, no one treatment or approach works best for everyone. Many of us require a combination of methods to feel the best we can. The challenge of emotional healing is how to find the practitioner and methods that work for you.

My solution has been to use the Dream Angel Meditation (chapter two) almost every night. During the meditation, I ask one question on what to do about a very real problem in my life. These problems can be related to feelings, family, work, and so on. The questions range from What should I do about my relationship with a coworker? to What am I so anxious about and what would help? to What school should my son go to next year? to What doctor should I see for a specific medical problem? etc. I ask the same question nightly until I get an answer.

This answer will appear in a dream or during the day as a clear intuition that I have come to know as the Voice of God. I say to myself, "Yes, of course, that's it!" These answers have led me to solutions to problems and also to the wonderful resources included in the Appendix on Emotional Healing. The meditations at the end of this chapter have been the most helpful for many people. Experiment with what helps you know the best path to develop an inner peace and joy.

Unlike Moshe in Rabbi Nachman's story, joy is not a constant for anyone. We need to practice and work to experience joy, just as we must practice and work to get the highest benefits from prayer. This is liberating because it gives us a method to feel so much better!

My brother Tom once told me a fable about life: Once there was a great emperor who wanted to know all of the wisdom in the world. He sent for the wisest men in his kingdom, paid them handsomely, and gave them one year to put all of this wisdom into ten books. At the end of the year, the emperor complimented their work and said, "I will pay you another great sum if, in one more year, you can put all of this wisdom into one book." This task was accomplished. Then the emperor said: "Another year, much more money, and I want the wisdom of the world in one sentence."

Each person I have told this story to has come up with her or his own sentence. The most common is: "Do unto others as you would have them do unto you." A very wise philosophy. What would your sentence be?

My brother's answer startled me because it was unexpected yet so true. The sentence that holds the wisdom of the world in Tom's fable is: "There is no free lunch." When you think about it, that's one of the great truths of the world—you get out of life the work that you put into it.

My choice for this one sentence is similar in meaning but further reaching: "What goes around, comes around." *Whatever* you do—good or bad—comes back to you.

I have learned that if I do my part, do the work—say the prayers, do the meditations, do good deeds, share my money—then God will not fail me. What goes around, comes around, especially with God. When you give, you get back in kind, and you also boost the efficacy of the Healing Prayer.

In Rabbi Nachman's story of Moshe, here is a man who lives the proverb: "Trust in the Lord with all your might. Do not depend on your own understanding. Acknowledge Him in all your ways; then He will direct your paths."

For me there are three lessons in this story: One is to have faith. The second is that when one is joyful, good things happen. And last, but by no means least: When one is joyful it spreads to others and then comes right back. Rabbi Nachman said, "Through depressions and sadness a man can forget who he really is. Therefore it is necessary to be continually in a state of joy, no matter what low level a person may be at. Through joy also, one can give renewed life to another. For there are people who suffer greatly and they walk around full of suffering and worry. When someone approaches them with a happy face he is able to give them renewed life. To do this is not some empty matter but an exceedingly great thing. . . ."

This is how I do my work and "body-build" my joy and faith:

1. I do the Healing Prayer and at least one meditation every day.

2. Something painful happens.

3. It usually takes a day or two for me to gather energy and reclaim joy.

4. I get going. One of my mottoes is: Get To Work!

5. The work is the prayer, meditations, and making sure that I am physically and emotionally on track.

6. Sometimes it is possible for me now to spontaneously have faith before the healing. Other times, I need to do the Greater Mind Meditation each time before the Healing Prayer and soon the faith is there.

7. I give of myself: time, energy, compassion, joy, and money.

8. I find a way to "move God." One must do something out of the ordinary to move God. For me it often is saying the Healing Prayer a number of times a day for a number of days with concentration and energy. This has been highly successful for me, but everyone should experiment with the prayer and discover what works for them.

9. I see the healing.

What a joyful experience! The Ba'al Shem Tov wrote, "When a person is happy, he unconsciously claps his hands. This is because his joy spreads through his entire body. The same is true of the Divine Presence. Each influence is transmitted to each of its parts."

The goal is joy! I love to watch three-year-olds bouncing down the street next to their tired parents. We have to reclaim that exuberance and spontaneity. During the Healing Prayer, experience the deepest, truest joy you know. Every day take a few moments and sit and visualize yourself joyful. Perhaps see yourself as an excited child getting birthday presents, running out to recess, or jumping into a swimming pool. Feel the thrill of a father swooping his toddler into the air. My deepest experience of joy was holding my laughing babies. These are the feelings to draw upon when saying the Healing Prayer.

Celia Levinson, a member of our Healing Prayer Group, says about what she has learned: "How would it be to feel loved all the time, feel approval, feel comfort, be encouraged to do difficult tasks, and then feel wonderful after I have accomplished the job? This is what visualizing, praying and meditating according to Rabbi Douglas's directions have done for me. A special feeling comes into me. There is a lovely, a very bouncy emotion that comes with the confidence that I am part of all creation."

How to Do It

MEDITATIONS TO BRING JOY

RABBI
DOUGLAS

A healing meditation based on the teachings of Rabbi Nachman of Bratslav

1. Find a comfortable and restful place in which you are not likely to be disturbed. Make yourself comfortable, loosening any tight-fitting clothing. Put a candle in a candle holder, light it, and do the Candle Meditation (page 14). Feel yourself filled with the light of God. When there is no separation between you and God, you are one with God. You are in the Greater Mind. Then

2. repeat the following words: "Through the Power of the Greater Mind, I feel happiness and joy which is mine."

3. Visualize something in your life which gives you joy. Meditate on it, and enjoy it. Repeat the following words: "I will that the joy and happiness that I feel now be with me all day."

A healing meditation based on the teachings of Rabbi Dan Dresher
Here is a meditation that will help you bring joy to others:

1. Find a comfortable and restful place in which you are not likely to be disturbed. Make yourself comfortable, loosening any tight-fitting clothing. Do the Candle Meditation.

2. When you are filled with the Light of God, stretch out your arms to receive more light from the heavens, as we did in chapter five. Catch two rays of light and pour the light on someone you know who is depressed. Repeat the following words, "Through the power of the Greater Mind, I pray El Na Rifa Na La." As you repeat this prayer, visualize your friend full of joy and happy, free from depression and melancholy.

3. At this point, you will yourself feel joyous because you are sharing joy with your friend. Visualize your friend happy and recite, "I will that the joy and happiness I feel now overflow and bring healing to _____."

Color meditation to create a feeling of joy

1. Choose a location where you are not likely to be interrupted. Either lie down or sit in a chair whose back is high enough to support your head.

2. Close your eyes and for a moment be totally aware of your intake and outflow of breath without making any attempt to control this process. Allow yourself to be aware of the total calmness which begins to flow through your entire body and mind.

3. Allow your inner mind to be fully saturated with the color blue. I personally focus on a sky blue. Rabbi Dresher taught me that in the Torah, the ancient Israelites are said to have made their prayer shawls with the color blue, reflecting the unlimited sky. This teaches us of unending hope, and that the color blue resembles the Infinite whom we want to enter us.

   Allow this blue image to fill every corner of your mind, feel a sense of tranquility and happiness. Imagine the air being a light, fluffy blue.

4. As you take a deep breath through your nostrils, imagine or visualize that you are pulling blue light into yourself and that this blue light is circulating throughout your entire body, calming your entire body and mind. Repeat this exercise three times, allowing yourself to be totally aware of the complete calmness in your mind and body as your mind's eye is conscious of the blueness flowing throughout your entire body and filling your mind completely. Feel Rabbi Nachman's sense of joy as you are conscious of a beautiful blueness in your body.

5. Open your eyes and go about your normal activities.

The Holiness Code

The Lord spoke to Moses, saying:

Speak to the whole Israelite community and say to them:

You shall be holy, for I, the Lord your God, am holy.

You shall each revere his mother and his father, and keep My sabbaths:

I the Lord am your God.

Do not turn to idols or make molten gods for yourselves: I the Lord am your God. . . .

When you reap the harvest of your land, you shall not reap all the way to the edges of your field, or gather the gleanings of your harvest.

You shall not pick your vineyard bare, or gather the fallen fruit of your vineyard; you shall leave them for the poor and the stranger; I the Lord am your God.

You shall not steal; you shall not deal deceitfully or falsely with one another.

You shall not swear falsely by My name, profaning the name of your God: I am the Lord.

You shall not defraud your neighbor. You shall not commit robbery. The wages of a laborer shall not remain with you until morning.

You shall not insult the deaf, or place a stumbling block before the blind. You shall fear your God: I am the Lord.

You shall not render an unfair decision: do not favor the poor or show deference to the rich; judge your neighbor fairly. Do not deal basely with your fellows. Do not profit by the blood of your neighbor. I am the Lord.

LEVITICUS 19:1–16

7: LET US MAKE MAN IN OUR IMAGE (GENESIS 1:26)

Universal Principle: Every person is created in the image of God

RABBI DOUGLAS   WHEN I first began praying with Rabbi Dresher, I felt somewhat awkward. It wasn't because I didn't believe in the healing power of God. It wasn't even because I was not an Orthodox Jew, as was Rabbi Dresher. It was because at first I thought Rabbi Dresher meant that God heals only those in whom He dwells, and that those who do not fill themselves up with the Presence of God, or those who are not filled with God, will not receive healing. I thought this meant that God lives in some, but doesn't live in others. Perhaps God lives only in Orthodox Jews, for example, and not in Lutheran Christians. This bothered me.

Later, this thinking also bothered Helen, a member of one of my prayer groups. She was troubled because she felt that my teachings maintain that if we don't do these meditations or meditations similar to these, we can't be filled up with the Presence of God. She suggested to me that God is everywhere, and His glory and Presence fill the universe, the trees and the rivers. Plants and animals are filled with God, as are sick and healthy people. Yet the trees don't do meditations, neither do many ill people in hospitals. Does that mean that God does not fill these people? Does this mean they are bereft of God? And does the Biblical text, "Let us make man in our image, after our likeness," (Genesis 1:26) mean, "Let us make only those who meditate in our image"?

I remember when I first shared my conflict about this with Rabbi Dresher. I wanted to know if God existed in my diseased body—when all the symptoms of Klippel-Trenaunay manifested themselves greatly. I was walking with a cane. I was lying on the floor with my leg up, even as I saw members of the synagogue for appointments. I was sitting on a chair to conduct services, rather than standing. I was told about the probability of amputation. But, I believed in Torah. I acted kindly toward my fellow man. I shared my money with people, as I have always done. But here was Rabbi Dresher teaching me to be and feel filled with the Presence of God. He said this would lead to my healing. Did he mean that my belief in Torah was not strong enough? Did he believe my sharing with others was not great enough? Did he honestly believe that God was not with me, and I was not good enough?

When I approached him and told him of the frustration I had, he reminded me of the magnificent text that Jews and Christians and Moslems and people of many other religions hold sacred, "Let us make man in our image, after our likeness."

He reminded me that just as God is holy, we should be holy. And he told me that holiness does not mean, as some of the classical Greeks thought, isolating oneself on Mt. Olympus—where the gods ate, loved, partied, and thought, and from where they ruled.

Mohammed, Moses, and Jesus teach that God is here on earth. This teaching is central to the Judeo-Christian ethic. Look at Leviticus 19. God says to the ancient Israelites: "You shall be a kingdom of priests, and each member of this kingdom shall be holy." And holiness for this text means giving honor to your parents, dealing with fairness in business, sharing money with a stranger, holding no grudges, showing the same respect to a deaf and blind person as you would to a sighted and hearing person, loving your neighbor as yourself, and such "ordinary" things.

When Rabbi Dresher showed me this text, he said, "When we behave with these principles, the Lord that is within all of us at birth, becomes activated." He then sent me to a marvelous Hebrew commentary on the Biblical verse, "Let us make man in our image." It's a mystical commentary, written by a tenth-century Italian Jewish scholar, Shabbetai Donnolo. It teaches us that all of us—Jew and Gentile— have God within us. If we understand the text and the commentary, we can see that for the God who is within us to work, we have to accept our partnership with God. We have to work together with God and activate the Divine Principle that is within us.

When I realized I had Klippel-Trenaunay in 1975, this did not mean that God was not within me. God was as much in me with Klippel-Trenaunay disease, as God is in the Reverend Billy Graham, the Pope, or the Chief Rabbi of Israel.

So, years later, I could share this thinking with Helen—just as the rabbi had shared this thinking with me. I told her that in order to turn on the God that was already within me, I had to incite God, excite God, inspire God. I had to breathe God within me even more strongly than I did before. I had to visualize the spirit of God moving within me from head to toe, like a river of light, with its many tributaries.

This situation can be compared to a room that is pitch black, dark as night, and yet the same room is wired for electricity. For the elec- tricity to function, we have to turn on the light switch. There is God in all people—diseased and well. But we have to turn on the God within all of us in order to allow the Spirit of God and the Breath of God to function at its highest.

When the Biblical Miriam was diseased with leprosy, this did not mean that she was without God. On the contrary, she was filled with God. She was among the few female prophets of the Hebrew Scriptures. But Moses had to turn on the switch within her. He had to turn on the light.

Now, Rabbi Dresher's home was in the Devon area of West Rogers Park, the most Jewish of Jewish areas in Chicago. This area abounds with Hasidic Jews of different persuasions. On Friday morning, you could see the Hasidic men and women coming out of the bakeries and bookstores. And on Saturday morning, you could see the streets of the community filled with Jews walking to synagogue.

Rabbi Dresher's apartment mirrored the ambiance of Devon Street. It was filled with books—books in bookcases, books on tables, books on his desk. On one table, there was a book called *Sefer Yetzirah*. He reached for it to illustrate his point that God is within all of us, but it is our duty to activate the God within us. I remember he told me, "Douglas, we are *shitufim*—partners with God. When there's a partnership, both partners work together. God works with you, and you work with God. And you build a business, the business of healthy living." Then he turned to Rabbi Donnolo's commentary on Genesis 1:26 in *Sefer Yetzirah*. The commentary shows how the health and welfare of a human body depends on one's breathing in the life force of God.

Donnolo implies that if we continually fill the human body with the Spirit of God, we remain in good health, and if the organs themselves are intact and in harmony with one another this increases the opportunity for the spirit of God to dwell in the body. Just as Isaac Luria and Rabbi Nachman of Bratslav maintain that it is easier for the Spirit of God to dwell in one who is joyful, Donnolo maintains that there is a correlation between health and the spirit of God. In his commentary to "Let us make man in our image, after our likeness," he says:

> All the time the body is whole and in good health, the breath of life will be in it, at the command of God, but if it is not complete and in good health, even lacking anything in any of the organs wherein is the breath of life, or if any of the organs are seriously diseased, or very painful, then, if because of the disease, and the pain, the limb or organ changes from its healthy state, then the breath of life, will experience great distress because it will not be able to remain in its original dwelling place in the original healthy body. . . . From this we know that the whole power of this lifeless mass to have a shape and sight and smell and swallowing and speech and to touch and to do and to have movement of limbs and to desire and have knowledge and understanding comes from the Spirit of the Breath of Life that the Maker and Creator breathed into us.

Here Donnolo not only says that a healthy body, where all the organs work in harmony with one another, depends on the Breath of the Spirit of Life, which is God. He also says that the continued functioning of the Breath of God depends on the harmonious healthy relationship of the organs of the body.

The organs of the body work in harmony with one another because every human body has a soul which enters a child at birth. The relationship between this soul and the body in which it is housed is crucial and very significant. Throughout the pages of this book, we have included meditations and meditative prayers that excite the soul and nourish the soul, so that the relationship between the body and soul becomes even stronger. When the soul is functioning at a high level— or when the soul drives the body to the best of its capacity—the body, its organs, and its many systems are very healthy. Donnolo speaks of the Breath of Life, which can be seen as meditative prayer that perfects the relationship between the soul and the body. When the soul and the body are in harmony with one another, there is health.

Rabbi Chaim Vital, a major disciple of Isaac Luria, and among the greatest Jewish Kabbalists ever, adds to our understanding of the direct relationship between body and soul in his great Kabbalistic text, *Sha'arei Kedushah: Gates of Holiness.* The body, he teaches, is not who the person is. The essential person is the soul. The soul consists of 248 "spiritual limbs and organs" which are connected by 365 spiritual strands.

> The body is a garment in which the intelligent soul, which is the man himself, clothes itself while he is in this world. . . . Just as a craftsman makes a bodily garment to cover the limbs of the body, so God creates Man's body which is the garment of his soul to cover the soul's 248 limbs and their 365 spiritual strands, which connect the limbs and serve as a conduit for the blood from limb to limb, like a spiritual pipe system. Then, after the formation of the body, God breathed into it the living soul with its 248 spiritual limbs and 365 spiritual strands. The limbs of the soul carry out their work through their instruments, the limbs of the body, which are like an axe in the hand of the person using it to hew. And, the proof of this is that the limbs of the body are not able to do their work, except while the soul is within them, the eye sees and the ear hears only when the soul is there. But when the

soul leaves, seeing is darkened and all sensation departs from the 248 limbs.

I spent nearly nine months praying with and studying under Rabbi Dan Dresher. And I must say it took almost that long before I could conduct services in my temple standing up, and not sitting in a special chair that the temple had bought for me. Even though I saw Rabbi Dresher once a week, every week, there were weeks when my condition was much worse, and it appeared as if I was not getting better at all. Or, just when I felt things were getting much better, I would have a relapse.

One day, when I was very despondent, Rabbi Dresher said, "Today, we are not going to pray. We are going to study from one of the greatest scholars since the time of Moses." And he pointed to his big volumes of Jewish law that were in brown bookcases facing us. I was wondering why he was showing me Joseph Caro's monumental work, the *Shulkhan Aruch*, the code of Jewish law.

Joseph Caro (1488–1575) is known and receives his pre-eminence among legal scholars as the author of the sixteenth century *Shulkhan Aruch*. The *Shulkhan Aruch* became the ultimate code of Jewish law. It is a summary of the *Beit Yosef,* in which Caro investigated every single law of Talmud, analyzed a multiplicity of divergent views, and finally arrived at decisive rulings. The *Shulkhan Aruch* has become the authoritative code of Jewish law for Orthodox Judaism around the world.

I knew that it is one of the Jewish *mitzvot* (laws) to be happy, but that day I was unhappy. So I said to Rabbi Dresher, "I know Jewish law requires us to be happy. When we are happy, our faith is more solid, we enter into a special relationship with God. But today, I'm not feeling very good."

Rabbi Dresher knew that I loved Torah and Kabbalah. He also knew that I enjoyed when he taught me Donnolo's commentary to Genesis 1:26. So he said, "I know you know that Rabbi Joseph Caro was a legal genius. But did you know that he was also a brilliant Kabbalist, writing mystical works even before Isaac Luria?"

Before I could answer, he told me of a secret mystical diary that

Joseph Caro wrote and kept. During a period of about fifty years, while Caro lived in the city of Safed, he wrote a secret diary called *Maggid Meshirim*. The diary was a collection of writings that included the visits of a *maggid*, a heavenly teacher, who instructed Rabbi Caro on mystical matters of law and Torah. This *maggid* introduced himself, using different names, such as "The Redeeming Angel," or "The Heavenly Mother," or even "The *Shekhina*." Usually he identified himself as the "Soul of the *Mishnah*," the first part of the Talmud, the Oral Law.

Joseph Caro would sit at his desk and a voice would come out of his mouth which he claimed was a visitation by the *maggid*. Caro wrote these visitations down in his mystical text, *Maggid Meshirim*. This diary is an excellent synthesis of Kabbalistic thought before the advent of Lurianic Kabbalah.

Rabbi Dresher then showed me Caro's wonderful mystical commentary on the same verse that Donnolo interpreted, "Let us create Man in our image." He said, "Let's study this now because this mystical commentary teaches how we can achieve joy in this world." And that's what I needed at that time.

"Let us make man in our image after our likeness." (Genesis 1:26). And this is the mystery of "and God said 'Let us make man in our image, after our likeness.'" God [*Elohim*] which is Binah said to the Ten *Sefirot*, 'Let us make man, that is: let every one of us produce one light and through the combination of all 10 lights, let us make man. "Man" that is *Matronitha*, as it is written, "According to the beauty of a man that it may remain in the house," (Isaiah 44:13) and it is the woman that remains in the house. And this man should be in our image . . . he is composed like us of 10 *Sefirot* . . . when Binah said, "let us make man," these lights combined and this man was born (Adam) who was in the likeness of a female whose limbs correspond to those of the male . . . when the Ten *Sefirot* of the *Matronitha* unite with the Ten Supernal *Sefirot*, they then correspond to each other and there is perfect union and joy in all the worlds. . . . This is the mystery of union which we have to perform always. And this is also the mystery of God making a woman of Adam's rib. Just as the *Shekhina* was produced by the movement of the 10 supernal *Sefirot*, which are the male world. And from the breath of life of God came into existence the body which symbolizes the 10 supernal *Sefirot*. And from this body of Adam was formed the female, which symbolizes the *Matronitha*, who was formed from the 10 *Sefirot*. . . . For each *Sefira* gave her one light and all these 10 lights combined and became one and this is the *Shekhina*. . . . This is the mystery of the True Doctrine which the Holy One, blessed be He, reveals to you."

In this text we see that the Divine Being is both feminine and masculine, and that it is our duty to bring together God's feminine and masculine aspects. Indeed, the Scripture says, "On that Day the Lord shall be One and His name One." That day will be a Messianic time pervaded with joy in the heavens and earth.

I realized that what Rabbi Dresher was sharing with me was that since all of us are created in the image of God, we, like God, have masculine and feminine aspects within us. When we are alive to our own femininity, and also alive to and are comfortable with our own masculinity, this brings joy. We can do our parts in bringing together the Upper World and Lower Worlds, heaven and earth—and, most importantly, the feminine and masculine aspects in God and in us—by remembering that we are all created in God's image.

Liberating Concept: I can be more like God even in the mother role!

MELINDA   One night as my sister, Mary Anne, and I were talking on the phone, we were simultaneously cleaning up spilled food, checking homework assignments, finding lost gloves, and telling kids to get ready for bed. We laughed and wondered how we stay sane and how we ever get anything done for ourselves.

Every time I sit down to write, one of my children shows up. Even though it has never been scientifically researched, without a doubt children have a "mother-doing-something-for-herself" inborn radar center in their brains. I can be home all day doing laundry and such, but the moment my computer goes on, my kids are there. They can be outside playing ball for an hour but this inborn radar says, "She's sitting down. Time to go in."

A large part of parenthood is the nitty gritty of often putting aside one's own needs and turning with pleasure to welcome the child. This is the response that defines the relationship. It is the look in the parent's eyes that says, "I think you are wonderful and I am happy to see you."

I always say about the time at home: I never get anything done but it is the most important thing that I do. After my husband has been with the kids all day, he looks the way I often feel. He has a slightly crazed look in his eye and babbles things like, "I didn't get anything done! I cleaned up the kitchen five times! They played in the snow all day and we changed clothes ten times!" We laugh together. My husband has named this the "mother role." He freely admits that this role is the hardest thing he does. It is a role that applies to anything people do when their time is not their own because others' needs are the top priority. It could easily be called the "rabbi role," the "ER doctor role," the "father role," or the "fireman role."

I often trade "horror" stories about loss of sanity with other parents. A friend with two-and-a-half-year-old twins one day desperately needed to close her eyes while her girls played right next to her. She awoke a few minutes later to the sight and sounds of her naked toddlers running and sliding across a wet kitchen floor. They had taken off their clothes and emptied a bucket of water and now were having the time of their lives! She was exhausted and had to clean up the kitchen and dry and dress two squealing girls. When she told me the story, we laughed until we cried. How can anything be so wonderful and so terrible at the same time!

The goal is to be more like God even though I can't get a grip. Monks and ascetics can live on a mountaintop and pray and meditate alone. The key word is alone. I am never alone even when I am by myself. My family never leaves my mind. Living in this world and being spiritual is a challenge. I call this part of the chapter: "'Hey Mom? Hey Mom!' How to be more like God even when in the Mother role."

To be more like God and to activate God to the highest degree, we have to bring together the physical and spiritual parts of ourselves. Just having a place to check off small accomplishments gave me incentive to do more.

I decided to set the following goals:

1. Emotional Goal: To think positively. The best technique I have ever found for changing from negative to positive thinking is in Anthony Robbins' book, *Awaken the Giant Within: How to take immediate control of your mental, emotional, physical & financial destiny!* In chapter thirteen, "The Ten-Day Mental Challenge," he details methods that are simple and effective.

2. Physical Goals: To exercise three times a week, to drink five glasses of water a day; and to eat five servings of fruits and/or vegetables a day.

3. Spiritual Goals: To say the Healing Prayer three times every day, to visualize the Light within me, and to visualize my loved ones well during the day; and to practice visualization for ten minutes every day.

4. The last goal on the chart below is a personal one—set your own according to what you want to change in your life.

Here is my goals chart for twenty days:

Days 1–10

	SAT 1	SUN 2	MON 3	TUES 4	WED 5	THURS 6	FRI 7	SAT 8	SUN 9	MON 10
AR 10 day	✓①	✓②	x	①	②	x	①	②	③	④
HP ③	✓✓✓	✓	✓	✓✓	✓✓	✓✓	✓✓	✓✓	✓✓	✓✓
Vis 10'	✓①	✓②	✓③	✓④	✓⑤	✓⑥	✓⑦	✓⑧	✓⑨	✓⑩
Water ⑤	✓✓	✓✓✓✓	✓✓	✓✓✓✓	✓✓✓	✓✓✓	✓✓	✓✓✓	✓✓✓	✓✓✓✓
F/V ⑤	✓✓	✓✓✓	✓✓	✓✓✓	✓✓✓✓			✓✓	✓	
Rem Vis	✓✓✓	✓✓	✓✓	✓✓✓	✓✓✓	✓✓		✓✓	✓	✓
En		✓			✓		✓	✓		
NA ✓①	✓②	✓③	✓④	⑤	✓⑥	x	①	②	③	④

Days 11–20

	TUES	SAT	SUN	MON	TUES	WED	THURS	FRI	SAT	SUN
	1	2	3	4	5	6	7	8	9	10
AR 10 day	⑤	⑨	⑩	⑪	⑫	⑬	⑭	⑮	⑯	⑰
HP ⑤	✓✓	✓✓	5★ ✓✓✓✓	✓✓✓ ✓✓✓	✓✓✓ ✓✓	✓✓✓ ✓✓	✓✓✓ ✓✓	✓✓ ✓✓	✓✓ ✓✓	✓✓ ✓✓
Vis 10'	⑪ 	 ✓				①	⑤ ✓ ✓		✓	✓ ✓
Water ⑤		 ✓✓✓✓	 ✓✓✓	 ✓✓✓✓	✓✓✓ ✓✓	✓	✓✓✓ ✓✓✓	✓✓ ✓✓	✓✓✓	✓✓✓✓
F/V ⑤	✓✓✓✓	✓	✓✓	✓✓	✓	✓✓✓	✓✓✓	✓✓✓ ✓✓	✓	✓✓✓
Rem Vis picture			✓✓ ✓✓✓✓	✓✓✓ 	✓✓✓ ✓	✓✓✓ ✓	✓✓✓ ✓	✓✓✓ ✓	✓✓✓ ✓✓	✓✓✓ ✓
En			✓				✓	✓		
NA	⑤	x	①	②	③	④	⑤	x	x	①

You can see that the goals were never completely met. In fact, if you look closely, you will also see that I skipped days twelve, thirteen, and fourteen. And this was a relatively calm time in my life! It did not matter because by just doing the best I could, I began to feel better.

On day thirteen, I changed one goal. I began a more intensive prayer for someone. This technique has been extremely successful for me. Again, this is something that I can *do*, when life is overwhelming or painful. As hard as it is to wait to see results, it is also difficult to set aside the time (even five minutes!) and calm down one's mind while doing the prayer. For years my "Western" mind kept saying, "Hurry up. There is so much to do. You're not getting anything done!" Our culture seems to idealize, "More is better." With practice, I have been able to refocus my thinking about the prayer to "This is the most important thing I will do today." And it is.

Barbara Melnick, a member of the Healing Prayer Group, says of her experience: "Healing prayer with Rabbi Douglas and Melinda has truly saved my life. On November 18, 1997, I was diagnosed with breast cancer. A tiny, six-centimeter, tumor was so aggressive that it grossly invaded seven lymph nodes. After a modified radical mastectomy, I had aggressive chemotherapy followed by radiation daily for six weeks. I will be on tamoxifen for the next five years. The past year was both horrible and beautiful. The tremendous emotional and spiritual problems seemed impossible. I look at Healing Prayer as part of my treatment. Prayers are part of my daily life. It has become a habit, like brushing my teeth and taking tamoxifen. I began the Prayer Group feeling horrible—sick, bald, frightened, and worried about dying. At first, I started feeling better spiritually. Then I started feeling better emotionally. Finally, I started feeling better physically. I know that I am with G-d; G-d is with me; I am protected; I am never alone; I am well; and, I am grateful and happy. I have framed יהוה [the Hebrew letters for YHVH] at work and at home. Each morning, before I go to work, I pray. I focus on the Hebrew letters and say the Healing Prayer. I envision myself well and cancer-free. I feel heat in my hands and chest during prayer times. I feel energy, love, and the presence of G-d. When I have free moments during the day, I repeat the prayers. When I go to bed at night, I pray again. The morning and night prayers are about ten minutes and the daytime prayers are about five minutes. A caring love developed among group members. We encourage each other. Each of us is blessed to be part of the group. Healing Prayer works."

In addition to working the prayer into our days, there is another requirement for the prayer to be successful. It is not enough to be able to say the prayer well and often. As Rabbi Douglas always reminds us, we must also be good people. Each religious tradition emphasizes this. For this prayer to work, we must do good works and be generous with money and ourselves.

We must *do* everything possible to be in the image of God. God created us in Her image and becoming more like God is our ongoing task to ensure the success of Her creation. We are partners with God. God has given us in Her Scripture a blueprint for achieving this. It is the Holiness Code which appears at the beginning of this chapter.

Another model of being more God-like is found in my favorite prayer, which is attributed to St. Francis of Assisi:

Lord, make me an instrument of your peace.
Where there is hatred, let me sow love;
Where there is injury, pardon;
Where there is doubt, faith;
Where there is despair, hope;
Where there is darkness, light;
Where there is sadness, joy;
Oh divine Master, grant that I may not so much seek
To be consoled as to console,
To be understood as to understand,
To be loved as to love;
For it is in giving that we receive;
It is in pardoning that we are pardoned;
It is in dying that we are born into eternal life.

One of my favorite people from my youth was a newly ordained Redemptorist priest who taught religion to my high school sophomore class. Father Dan had a radiant smile and a warm, gentle nature. He always had time to talk to young teens. I can still picture him surrounded by chattering students. He lived what he taught. He said that one must always strive to be without sin but, even more importantly, one must do good for others. He challenged us to always remember Jesus' words: Whatever you do to the least of my brothers, you do onto me.

"For I was hungry and you gave me food, I was thirsty and you gave me something to drink, I was a stranger and you welcomed me, I was naked and you gave me clothing, I was sick and you took care of me, I was in prison and you visited me." (Matthew 25: 35–36). "Truly I tell you, just as you did it to one of the least of these who are the members of my family, you did it to me." (Matthew 25:40)

Again, we can become more God-like bit by bit. Saint Thérèse of Lisieux wrote in *The Little Way*, "I have always desired to become a saint, but in comparing myself with the saints I have always felt that

I am as far removed from them as a grain of sand, trampled under-
foot by a passer-by, is from the mountain whose peak is hidden in the
clouds." She received her consolation from the Scriptures in the Book
of Proverbs: "Whoever is a little one, let that person come to me
(Proverbs 9:4)." (Obviously she made it to sainthood!)

Shinichi Suzuki, in his book, *Nurtured by Love: A New Approach to
Education,* writes about music education as a way for children to
develop into people with fine and pure hearts. He says that it is not
enough to play the violin well. Children need to develop both splendid ability and a noble mind with a high sense of values. The ultimate
goal is to make the child "splendid in mind and heart also."

On day seventeen I added a new goal: to use one of Dr. Suzuki's
techniques. I decided that in each Healing Prayer, I would visualize
the Hebrew letters five times in a row in at least one part of the prayer
without a major thought interruption.

I highly recommend Dr. Suzuki's book. He is concerned with not
only what we should become but also *how to do it* (some of my favorite
words). He writes, "To make a resolution and act accordingly is to live
with hope. Confronted with a high mountain, one cannot reach the
summit in one stride, but must climb step by step to approach one's
goal. . . . Do not hurry. This is a fundamental rule. If one hurries and
collapses or tumbles down, nothing is achieved. Do not rest in your
efforts; this is another fundamental rule. Without stopping, without
haste, carefully taking a step at a time forward will surely get you there.
To commit oneself to untiring patience and strong endurance, what
we call *kan*—intuition or sixth sense—is an absolute necessity in education." He believes that one can *learn* (another of my favorite words)
intuition. "Through repeated practice we acquire remarkable strength.
Our life activity involuntarily works up a great power, namely the ability of *kan* that enables us to overcome all difficulties." Dr. Suzuki says
that it is not true that one is born with intuition. "To foster intuition—
kan—there is no other way than sincere training." And the road to *kan*
comes from *doing*, what he calls the "habit of action." This habit of
action "is the most important thing we must acquire. Life's success or

failure actually depends on this one thing. So what should we do? We should get so that it is second nature to put our thoughts into action." If you have ever seen a performance by Suzuki's young students, you know the possibilities in his philosophy.

Being God-like is not just the large things we do or do not do, or even the prayer we say or do not say. Our lives are made up of countless moments where we can be kind, open, giving and available. I was eloquently reminded of this when my brother, Phil Arant, a devout Christian, sent me a collection of his poems. Phil and his wife, Nancy, have five wonderful children. In his poem, "The Book," Phil writes about the "father role":

> I hold this book within my hands
> And orchestrate some careful plans
> To enjoy these contents all alone
> Escape the loads which I bemoan
>
> I creep behind this careful place
> As children pass in heedless race
> They do not see my covert quest
> To find this secret time of rest
>
> There they leave, it's safe I hope
> To speed to world in which I cope
> A world I enter in these pages
> Of noble knights and wise old sages
>
> I find still room and lock the door
> And grasp my world of thoughts galore
> The chair so soft and soul such rest
> How can I tell how I am blest
>
> Yet as I drift into far places
> Two daughters appear from hidden spaces
> With shouts "Surprise" and leap on lap
> With careful plans their dad to trap

My drifting pose now shattered full
And now my book they try to pull
To free it from its guarded place
And be in center of my face

Again I sigh and let book fall
And out of bliss I somehow crawl
And hold my temper from these two
Who do not realize what they do

Contagious now the joy they share
My smile grows from source somewhere
I have on lap these gifts to see
And forgot which book was lent to me

How to Do It

TWO HEALING MEDITATIONS

RABBI
DOUGLAS   *A healing meditation affording general good health*

Here is a healing meditation based on Shabbetai Donnolo's commentary to "Let us make Man in our Image" (Genesis 1:26) and Levi Yitzchak's idea of the Greater Mind.

1. Find a comfortable, quiet and restful place which will become your regular place of meditation. Let this place be safe and secure for you. Make yourself comfortable by loosening your tie and other binding clothing. Close your eyes and breathe in the Breath of the Spirit of Life, the same breath that God breathed into Adam at his creation. Experience this breath flowing through your entire body, traveling and spreading through you. Feel the Breath of Life going through your head, your chest area, your stomach, your arms, your legs, and then up again and out through your nostrils. As this breath

is traveling through you, feel it or even visualize it. (When I pray for general health and not the cure of a specific ailment, I visualize the Breath of the Spirit as a yellowish light coursing through my body.) Feel relaxed and confident and reach for the Greater Mind.

2. When you are in the state of Greater Mind, visualize your circulatory system—including your blood vessels and arteries and veins throughout your body. Visualize the flow of blood moving smoothly throughout your body. Now you articulate the following words, "I am in the Greater Mind. I will that my circulatory system work perfectly, bringing life to all the cells of my body. I will that my circulatory system be in complete harmony with all other systems of my body."

3. In your mind's eye, visualize your lungs. Watch the lungs as they expand to take in air and contract to expel impurities from your body. Articulate the following words to yourself silently, "I am in the Greater Mind. I will that my respiratory system work perfectly, taking in oxygen and carrying oxygen to every part of my body. I will that my respiratory system be in complete harmony with all other systems of my body."

4. In your mind's eye, visualize your digestive system. See an image of your stomach and small intestines and large intestines. Repeat the following words to yourself, "I am in the Greater Mind. I will that my digestive system work perfectly, making good use of all the food in my body. I will that my digestive system be in complete harmony with all other systems of my body."

5. In your mind's eye, visualize your heart. See the heart working well. Repeat the following words to yourself, "I am in the Greater Mind. I will that my heart work well. I will that my heart be in complete harmony with all other systems of my body."

6. In your mind's eye, visualize your skeletal system. Visualize your bones and joints and tendons and muscles. Repeat the following words to yourself, "I am in the Greater Mind. I will that all the

bones and joints and tendons and muscles of my body work perfectly. I will that my bones and joints of my body be in complete
harmony with all other systems of my body."

7. In your mind's eye, see yourself as the picture of perfect health.
Visualize all the systems of your body working in harmony with one
another, as the Breath of the Spirit of Life, given by God, flows
harmoniously and gently throughout every organ and system of your
body. Create any vision or picture that feels good. Recognize that
all this healing and goodness is from God. Repeat the following
words to yourself, "I am in the Greater Mind. In the Greater Mind,
I am One with God, and my will can do anything. I will that all
systems of my body and mind be in complete harmony inside themselves and in relation to each other. I am in perfect health in mind
and body. Through the miracle of healing and the power of the
Greater Mind, I am and shall continue to be a perfectly healthy
human being." Open your eyes and go about your daily activities.

Healing meditiation based on Joseph Caro's **Maggid Meshirim,** *uniting*
Adam Kadmon and the **Shekhina** *(Divine Presence)*

The feminine aspect of God is called, in Hebrew, the *Shekhina*, and
she is represented by the *Sefira* Malchut. Her color is blue. In order
to bring joy not only to the world, but to ourselves, we want to unify
the *Shekhina* with the ten Supernal *Sefirot*. These ten supernal *Sefirot*
can be visualized as Adam Kadmon or the masculine presence of God.

1. Do the Candle Meditation from page 14. When you feel yourself
filled with the light of God, you will be ready for the next step,
which is to visualize Adam Kadmon with his many colors. This is
very enjoyable.

2. There is a Jewish *midrash* that teaches that when God created the
first human man, he created Adam from the earth of the four cor-
ners of the world, using red earth, green earth, black earth, and
brown earth, so that no man would later rise up and say, "My race
is better than yours." In the same way, Adam Kadmon or Man's

spiritual counterpart—God's blueprint for creating Man—indeed symbolically, the male aspect of God, can be visualized as a multicolored being.

See the multi-colored Adam Kadmon. Look at the colors of the many-colored *Sefirot* comprising Adam Kadmon (see figure page 107). Malchut is royal blue, Yesod is white and red, Hod is dark pink, Netzach is light pink, Tiferet is purple, Chesed is white and silver, Gevurah is red and gold, Binah is green, Chochmah is sky blue, and Keter is white.

3. If you are a woman, feel the joy of being a woman. If you are a man, celebrate your feminine nature or the feminine aspect of God. Now move up the *Sefirot* and let the *Shekhina* and her blueness coalesce with Yesod and let Yesod welcome the Blue *Shekhina*. The *Shekhina* is embraced next by Netzach and Hod, where the colors of light pink and dark pink give way to blue. Feel the joy within you as you bring together the feminine and masculine aspects of God.

Continue to visualize Adam Kadmon as he receives His *Shekhina*, occupying the place of Tiferet where purple gives way to a royal blue. The transformation continues as Chesed and Gevurah welcome *Shekhina* and become blue. And now, joyfully, let the *Shekhina* come together with Binah, Chochmah, and Keter so that when you visualize Adam Kadmon/*Shekhina*, you now see Him/Her as a royal blue.

4. Gaze on the Adam Kadmon/*Shekhina* figure and inhale the blue within the pores of your body. Allow a wave of blue to fill every pore of your body from head to toe. You are filled with a warm, royal sensation of blue, and you are joyful because you have united, through your Greater Mind, with faith, the feminine and masculine aspects of God, and you have brought the Presence of God within you.

8: ALTERNATIVE MEDITATIONS

Universal Principle: The Power of the Name of God

RABBI DOUGLAS THE HEBREW language is very sacred. According to Jewish tradition, inherent in each letter are electric-like forces that God used to create the Universe. These Hebrew letters provide us with the foundation for many healing meditations, some of which we will explore here in some detail. Even though these Hebrew letters may be foreign to many of our readers, I urge you not to skip over this material nor to feel intimidated by it. Throughout Jewish history, many "healing rabbis" have used the amazing power of these secret letters to effect healing. In this chapter, the veil of secrecy is to some degree removed, and the power of the letters is unleashed. This material is accessible to everyone.

When I was a boy, though both my grandfathers were Orthodox rabbis, they never spoke Hebrew outside the synagogue. When they spoke to my Mom or Dad or their friends, they would speak Yiddish, and when they spoke to me, they would speak in English. When I was seven years old, I attended an Orthodox parochial school, Young Israel of Montreal, and there I was first introduced to the Hebrew language.

One evening, in 1952, I came home and my mother's father, Rabbi Abraham Sheinman, was speaking Yiddish to my mom. I asked him why he was not speaking in Hebrew, especially since I had just learned in school that day that the Jewish people now have a Jewish homeland with Hebrew as our national language. He said to me, "Religious Jews shouldn't speak in Hebrew. We should speak in English or Yiddish. We should only use Hebrew in the synagogue [in prayer], not in the streets. Hebrew is *lishon ha-kodesh*."

He explained to me that *lishon ha-kodesh* is translated as "the holy tongue" and is another term for the Hebrew language. Jewish tradition teaches that the world was created with the twenty-two letters of the Hebrew alphabet (below). The *Zohar*[1] says, "For when the world was created, it was the supernal letters that brought into being all the work of the lower world, literally after their own pattern. Hence, whoever has a knowledge of them and is observant of them is beloved both on high and below." Not only are these letters sacred and holy, but the letters are forces of nature, instruments that God uses to continually create worlds.

LAMED
HAS THE SOUND OF L

ALEPH
SILENT LETTER

MEM
HAS THE SOUND OF M

BET / VET
HAS THE SOUND OF B OR V

NUN
HAS THE SOUND OF N

GIMEL
HAS THE SOUND OF G

SAMEKH
HAS THE SOUND OF S

DALET
HAS THE SOUND OF D

AYIN
SILENT LETTER

HEY
HAS THE SOUND OF H

PEY / FEY
HAS THE SOUND OF P OR F

VAV
HAS THE SOUND OF V

TZADI
HAS THE SOUND OF TZ

ZAYIN
HAS THE SOUND OF Z

QOPH
HAS THE SOUND OF K

CHET
HAS THE SOUND OF CH

RESH
HAS THE SOUND OF R

TET
HAS THE SOUND OF T

SHIN / SIN
HAS THE SOUND OF SH OR S

YOD
HAS THE SOUND OF Y

TAV
HAS THE SOUND OF T

KAPH / KHAPH
HAS THE SOUND OF K OR KH

The Kabbalah maintains that ordinary languages *represent* reality; their letters and words represent objects. This is not so with the holy tongue of Hebrew. The Hebrew letters are themselves the truest reality, immutable and eternal like the forces of nature. For example, the Hebrew letters for "sefer" (book), ספר —*samek fay resh*—represent the forces of nature that give books their real world existence. While the English word "book" is only a symbol for the concrete book, in the Hebrew language, letters of the alphabet are the very building blocks with which the world was and is created.

Perhaps the oldest known Kabbalistic work is a text called *Sefer Yetzirah*. It is so old that Moses Cordovero, in his magnum opus *Pardes Rimonim*, maintained that *Sefer Yetzirah* was then so old that there were those who even earlier attributed its authorship to the patriarch Abraham. Other scholars, however, maintain that it was written during Talmudic times. (*circa* 300 BCE–400 CE)

The *Sefer Yetzirah* is a book of numbers and letters teaching that the world was created with ten numbers and the twenty-two letters of the Hebrew alphabet. The numbers are related to the ten *Sefirot* (see p. 105) and the letters are the natural powers or forces of nature. The *Sefer Yetzirah* is a unique, meditative text that abounds in mystical meditations that use divine names and letter permutations to reach higher states of consciousness. The author of *Sefer Yetzirah* writes:

> There are 22 foundation letters. God (He) engraved them. He carved them. He weighed them. He combined them. He permuted them. And He formed with them the soul of all that was created and the soul of all that will be created.

The Kabbalah, in explaining this text from *Sefer Yetzirah*, maintains that the letters in the text are alive—really alive—and they are related to all the organs and vessels of the human body. Therefore, establishing the correct relationship between the Hebrew letters and the organs and vessels within a person is very important. This is why we use these letters in healing prayer. The Jewish mystics taught us to visualize these letters in our mind with our inner eye and to meditate on these letters by writing them, visualizing them, and embracing and dancing with them as if they were living beings.

One specific meditative method is to take a word and permute it in all possible ways. When we do this, we divest the mind and soul of material and corporeal thought, and thus heighten our spiritual awareness. This can lead to our healing.

One unique word that the Jewish mystics have used with their various permutations is the *Tetragrammaton*. The *Tetragrammaton* is one of God's many names, and many consider it God's most holy name. During the Biblical period, on the Day of Atonement, the High Priest would enter the inner sanctum of the ancient temple and would pronounce aloud this holy name of God in prayer on behalf of the whole congregation of Israel. At least until the First Temple of the ancient Hebrew was destroyed in 586 BCE, this name was regularly pronounced with its proper vowels. Today, when we see this name, written as the consonants YOD HEY VAV HEY (the Hebrew Torah is written without vowels), and because the name is so holy, we Jews cannot accurately pronounce the YHVH name, as did the ancient priest. By the end of the third century BCE, the pronunciation of the holy name Yod Hey Vav Hey (YHVH) was avoided, and the word *Adonai*, the Lord, was substituted for it.

MEDITATIONS BASED ON THE יהוה TETRAGRAMMATON

The following meditations are "alternative meditations" that allow us to enter into a state of the Greater Mind so that when we pray for physical healing, we will be receptive to God's healing Presence. They are not in a specific order of difficulty or understanding. I have seen that each day I feel the Presence of God a bit differently and this feeling inspires me to do different meditations. There are times when I want to draw near to God; there are times when I want to dance with God. There are times that I want to yell at God; and, there are times that I want to become one with God. Included in this chapter are many meditations based on the יהוה (YHVH), allowing many different ways of approach to the Holy Name.

A SPIRITUAL MEDITATION BASED ON THE
SACRED NAME OF יהוה (YHVH)

Here is a meditation based on the permutation of this ancient, sacred
name of יהוה Yod Hey Vav Hey (YHVH). This mystical meditation
of twelve permutations of יהוה (YHVH) was widely practiced by the
Jewish mystics, including Cordovero and Rabbi Elijah Gaon of Vilna.
Moses Cordovero in his text *Pardes Rimonim* recites each consonant
of the יהוה (YHVH) in its twelve permutations. We do as he did,
and as we recite each consonant, we visualize the letter before us, recognizing that we are in the Presence of God, calling on His holy name.
When we do this meditation, we divest our mind and soul of the physical realities that surround us. Instead, we focus on, and bring within
us, the eternal forces of Nature that God has used and uses to create
this world. Indeed, we bring in God. We become one with God.
Healing begins!

Below is a chart with the twelve permutations of the יהוה (YHVH)
name of God. Please note that the Hebrew characters are written, and
read, from right to left, while the English characters are read from left
to right.

A note on pronunciation: Yod rhymes with good. Hey rhymes with
hay. Vav rhymes with love.

Recite the twelve permutations in the order as they are written
below. As you recite each permutation, visualize the letters. So, for the
first permutation, you recite Yod Hey Vav Hey as you visualize the four
respective letters. Recite these twelve names of God at your own speed,
but it is crucial that, as you recite the letters, you are completely focused
on your visualization of the letters.

י ה ו ה

YOD = י   HEY = ה   VAV = ו   HEY = ה

1. יהוה   Yod Hey Vav Hey
2. היוה   Hey Yod Vav Hey

3. ויהה   Vav Yod Hey Hey

4. הוהי   Hey Vav Hey Yod

5. יההו   Yod Hey Hey Vav

6. היהו   Hey Yod Hey Vav

7. והיה   Vav Hey Yod Hey

8. ההיו   Hey Hey Yod Vav

9. יוהה   Yod Vav Hey Hey

10. הויה   Hey Vav Yod Hey

11. וההי   Vav Hey Hey Yod

12. ההוי   Hey Hey Vav Yod

A MEDITATION BASED ON THE SHIVITI (PSALMS 16:8)

The *Shiviti* meditation is a classic Hebrew meditation that involves our gazing on the four letters of the Divine Name, יהוה (YHVH). We call this meditation a *Shiviti* meditation because this spiritual exercise is derived from verse 8 of Psalm 16: "I have set [*shiviti*] יהוה (YHVH) before me always."

First, we learn how to recognize the four Hebrew characters of the YHVH:

י ה ו ה

Know what a Yod looks like, a Hey looks like, a Vav looks like. As we look at the *Shiviti*, we enter its power and we are filled with the light of יהוה (YHVH). I have found that staring and gazing at יהוה can be very powerful in healing. Before you offer any prayer to God, focus on the יהוה (YHVH). See it before you, with a bright ray of light emanating from the Yod, another ray of light emanating from the Hey, a third ray of light emanating from the Vav, and a fourth ray of light emanating from the final Hey. The four rays of light converge on your chest. As you visualize this vision of God, recite as a *mantra* twelve times Psalm 16:8, "I have set יהוה [YHVH] before me always." Feel God's energy and presence filling you through God's holy letters.

A mystical meditation based on Chapter 2, Sefer Yetzirah *and the teachings of Moses Cordovero and Isaac Luria*

In this meditation, you will find yourself filled with God's presence through the use of the Holy Letters which make up the name of God.

1. Find a place that you will use every day. As mentioned earlier, it is most effective if you meditate or pray in the same place, at the same time every day. This practice brings a sense of stability and constancy to your prayer. We have seen that if you pray at a regular time in the same place, you are more likely to do your prayers regularly.

2. Sit in a comfortable chair. Don't cross your legs or your arms. Be in relaxed clothing and unbuckle your belt.

3. Recall the four Hebrew characters of the YHVH:

   ## יהוה

   These letters are God's forces of nature. They are miraculous.

4. Focus on the Yod י. Look at it. Gaze on it. Do the same with the Hey ה, the same with the Vav ו, and the same again with the Hey ה. And now permute this name in eleven more ways, using the diagram on pages 102–3. Visualize each of the letters as if they were right in front of you. See them dancing, jumping, skipping—these letters are alive, and the more life you can see in these letters, the more health and life you will have.

5. Feel that you are connected with Yod Hey Vav Hey יהוה, God, and go about your day, knowing that He is always with you. This meditation will give you a great sense of well-being and good health.

יהוה *(YHVH) meditation*

As in the previous meditation, sit in the comfortable chair you will use every day for these exercises, don't cross your arms or legs, be in relaxed clothing, unbuckle your belt, loosen your tie, etc. Recall the four Hebrew letters of יהוה (YHVH), then

1. Hold a sheet of paper or a card in front of you which has the twelve Hebrew permutations of God's Holy Name יהוה (YHVH) as given on pages 102–3 in this book.

2. Read these twelve permutations out loud, focusing on each letter and thinking only of these letters and nothing else. Don't think of your children coming home from school. Don't think of the boss's assignment. Don't think of the ringing telephone. Only think of these holy letters. Look at them. Stare at them. Recite them aloud, in the order of these twelve permutations.

3. Try to do this with your eyes closed. Cheating is allowed and encouraged. Open your eyes and look at the letters. Close your eyes and visualize them. Eventually you will know them by heart. But for now, it's perfectly fine to look at the letters on the card which you are holding in front of you.

4. Now, here is what makes this exercise so different from the one on page 102. *Breathe in* each of the individual letters, one at a time, within each of the twelve permutations, so that you and the letters of God are one. You will do this exercise, breathing in each letter of each permutation. There are four letters in each permutation; there are twelve permutations. Understandably, this spiritual exercise is long, but that's the point. When you are focused on the Hebrew letters of the name of God, to the exclusion of all other things around you, you will then be immersed with the Presence of God.[2] You and God are one. Healing has already begun.

• • •

The Jewish mystics have always encouraged our focusing on the *Tetragrammaton*. The *Tetragrammaton* relates to the ten *Sefirot*. The classic Kabbalistic text, the *Zohar* teaches that there are ten *Sefirot*. The *Sefirot* are Divine Powers or attributes of God. They are different aspects of God as they appear to humans. The Hebrew word *Sefirot* is the plural of *Sefira*. According to the Kabbalists, these *Sefirot* are ten Powers or Attributes within God that God uses to create the world.

Gershom Scholem in his book, *Kabbalah,* maintains that the Hebrew word *Sefira* is related to the Hebrew word *Sappir,* since it is the Radiance of God which is like that of the Sapphire. He also maintains that "The *Sefirot* both individually and collectively subsume the archetype of every created thing. Just as they are contained in the Godhead, so they impregnate every being outside it. Thus the limitation of their number to ten necessarily involves the supposition that each one is composed of a large number of such archetypes." Scholem says that most of the early Kabbalists accepted the view that the *Sefirot* are identical with God's Essence.[3]

Each *Sefira,* or attribute of God is given a name by the Kabbalists. These *Sefirot* are powers, forces, vitalities, virtues, attributes, principles, which were produced or unfolded from God's creative power. These ten *Sefirot* are also regarded as vessels and receptacles of Divine Power and its attributes.

The First *Sefira* is called *Keter* (Crown). This can be identified with the Will of God. The next two *Sefirot* are called *Chochmah* (Wisdom) and *Binah* (Understanding). Scholem maintains that these first three *Sefirot* represent the evolution from Will to Thought. The Fourth *Sefira* is *Chesed* (God's Compassion). The Fifth *Sefira* is *Gevurah* (God's Strict Judgment). The Sixth *Sefira* is called *Tiferet* (Beauty). The Seventh *Sefira* stands for *Netzach* (Lasting Endurance). The Eighth *Sefira* stands for *Hod* (Glory). The Ninth *Sefira* is called *Yesod* (Foundation), and the Tenth *Sefira* is called *Malchut* (Kingdom). This *Sefira* is also known as *Shekhina,* God's Feminine Presence. These ten *Sefirot* are not arithmetical numerals.

Now, the *Sefirot,* when visualized, are seen in three columns as shown on page 107. The right column or masculine column includes Chochmah, Chesed, and Netzach. The left column or feminine column includes Binah, Gevurah, and Hod. The central column passes from Keter through Tiferet to Yesod and finally to Malchut.

The unfolding of the *Sefirot* within God is a system of opposites. The right side represents expansion, liberalism, and increase, while the left side represents contraction, conservatism, and decrease. The middle *Sefirot* represent the balance between them.

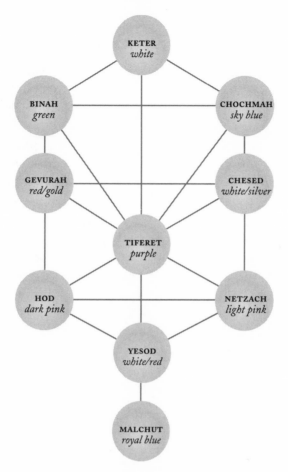

The Kabbalists believed and maintained that God is always One, that the ten Attributes or Powers don't symbolize ten intermediary beings, but only God. When one prays Kabbalistically, these ten Attributes or *Sefirot* within God are visualized as bright spheres of light.[4]

When we do Kabbalistic meditation on the *Sefirot,* we follow the way of the early and later Kabbalists. The Kabbalist would close his eyes and visualize each *Sefira* with its corresponding attributes or colors or Name of God. The Kabbalist would see, as we should see, the *Sefirot* dancing with one another, shining on one another, and combining with one another. When we do this, we connect ourselves to God's attributes; we connect ourselves to God. When we make God's *Sefirot* our own, God's powers become our own. Hence, meditations on the *Sefirot* inspire us and allow us to become one with God.

Moses Cordovero[5] understands that by gazing and focusing and contemplating on the mysterious letters יהוה (YHVH), one is brought into a close affinity and special relationship with God. He teaches in his book in Gate 19, Chapter 4, that while there are ten names corresponding to the ten *Sefirot*, there is one common name for all the *Sefirot*—the name of the *Tetragrammaton*, יהוה (YHVH). The Yod is Chochmah, the Hey is Binah, Vav is the six *Sefirot* and the final Hey is Malchut. The divine light shines and is spread within these four letters.[6]

The Hebrew language, like English, consists of consonants and vowels. So far, we have been speaking about the consonants and how God used these twenty-two consonants to create the universe. The Hebrew vowels are also mystical letters, even though they don't have the same force or power as the twenty-two consonants. Nonetheless, the vowels are also used in meditative practice. Unlike English, or any of the Romance languages, most of the Hebrew vowels are placed below the line and under the consonants. Here is a chart of the Hebrew vowels ("X" represents any Hebrew consonant for position only):

X	HAS THE SOUND OF EH	X	HAS THE SOUND OF EY
X	HAS THE SOUND OF AH	X	HAS THE SOUND OF AH
X	HAS THE SOUND OF EE	X	HAS THE SOUND OF IH
ןX	HAS THE SOUND OF OH	X	HAS THE SOUND OF OO
X	HAS THE SOUND OF OH	ןX	HAS THE SOUND OF OO

The ten *Sefirot* are associated with ten names. Each name is spelled with the four letters of the *Tetragrammaton*. The names are only differentiated by their vowels. I include a simple meditating table to illustrate Cordovero's thinking. The table on page 109 includes the ten *Sefirot*, their corresponding vowels, and the corresponding holy name of the *Tetragrammaton* and how it is pronounced.[7]

We meditate by first concentrating on the Yod Hey Vav Hey of

Keter (with its respective vowels), working all the way down to the Yod Hey Vav Hey of Malchut (which has no vowels), or, begin with Malchut and end with Keter.

It has been my experience that one does not have to pray in the "right order" of *Sefirot*. But as long as one concentrates and focuses on the יהוה (YHVH), with their respective vowels, one's mind begins the transformation from the Lesser Mind to the Greater Mind.

A Kabbalistic meditation on the Name of God, יהוה (YHVH) based on Moses Cordovero, Pardes Rimonim, Gate 19: Sha'ar Shem ben Dalet

As in the previous meditation, sit in the comfortable chair you will use every day for these exercises, don't cross your arms or legs, be in relaxed clothing, unbuckle your belt, loosen your tie, etc. Recall the four Hebrew letters of יהוה YHVH, then

1. Hold a sheet of paper or a card in front of you which has the ten different vocalizations of the YHVH name of God, shown below. You will recite the YHVH name of God with its ten vocalizations that correspond to the ten different *Sefirot*.

NAMES OF GOD	CORRESPONDING NAMES OF SEFIROT	
Hebrew	*English Transliteration*	
יְהֹוָה	Ya Ha Va Ha	Keter
יַהֲוָה	Ya Ha Va Ha	Chochmah
יֵהֵוֵה	Yey Hey Vey Hey	Binah
יֶהֶוֶה	Yeh Heh Veh Heh	Chesed
יִהִוִה	Yih Hih Vih Hih	Gevurah
יֹהֹוֹה	Yo Ho Vo Ho	Tiferet
יֵהֵוֵה	Yee Hee Vee Hee	Netzach
יֻהֻוֻה	Yu Hu Vu Hu	Hod
יֻהֻוֻהֻ	Yu Hu Vu Hu	Yesod
יהוה	Y H V H (no vowels)	Malchut

2. It's okay to look at the chart as you recite these names. Look
   at the chart. See God's name corresponding to Keter. Close
   your eyes. Visualize it. Do the same with God's name for all
   the ten *Sefirot.*

3. Cordovero allows you to begin with Keter and end with
   Malchut, or begin with Malchut and end with Keter. Rabbi
   Dresher believes you can begin with any of the *Sefirot,* just as
   long as you recite all the ten different pronounced names of the
   YHVH.

4. When you do this, you are allowing the Divine Light to shine
   within you. You are making contact with the inner light which
   is God. As you do this, you are filled up with the Presence of
   God and have within you the framework of the Kabbalah,
   entered through the Greater Mind.

5. At this stage you are free to do a healing meditation of your
   choice.

COLOR AND PRAYER

When my mother had colon cancer, we vigorously prayed with her,
using color visualization. The use of colors gave her a great feeling of
spirituality and enabled her to come closer to God.

The use of color and prayer was practiced by the Jewish mystics
of sixteenth-century Palestine, and even before. The great Kabbalist
Moses Cordovero discusses the importance and techniques of using
color in his encyclopedia of mysticism *Pardes Rimonim* in Chapter 10:
Sha'ar Ha-Gaveyneem, The Gate of Colors. In his concluding chapter,
Chapter 32: *Sha'ar Ha-Kavvanah,* he maintains:

> It is good and pleasant if one wishes to visualize the different
> vocalizations of the *Tetragrammaton* according to their colors,
> because then, without a doubt, a person's prayer will be extremely
> effective, on the condition that one's intention is that there is no
> other way in this world to compare the workings of a specific
> *Sefira,* except with a specific color. Since the colors are numerous

in the Gate of Colors [which we already discussed], we will not discuss the colors here, but when one wishes to direct one's prayer, look at the Gate which is before the eyes of the person praying.

Cordovero teaches here that successful prayer incorporates the use of colors. This is shown clearly in his Chapter 10, where we see the relationship between prayer, the *Sefirot*, and colors:

> In many places in Kabbalistic texts and in the *Zohar*, one finds that known colors parallel all the *Sefirot*. One must be very cautious and not think that this activity is to be taken literally. Color is something physical, and it is one of the attributes of physical properties, and that which is not physical, that is [the *Sefirot*], should not be described with physical properties. If one thinks that these are literally the colors of the *Sefirot*, he destroys the system and the boundaries established by the early mystics. Consequently, one who studies this should be very careful, but the colors compare to the functions that are drawn from the highest roots. . . . The color white teaches Mercy and Peace. This is because people who visit with white hair are merciful. For example, the elderly and the aged do not go to war. Therefore, if we wish to relate peace and the *Sefira* of Chesed (Compassion/Love), we relate it with the color White. And there is no doubt that white derives from the power of this root, as we explained earlier. This is the right understanding of the relationship between the colors and the *Sefirot*. The colors are used allegorically to relate to their functions and activities. . . . And there is no doubt that the colors serve as a gate to the functions of the *Sefirot*. Also, they carry influences from the different *Sefirot*. . . .

Cordovero also maintains:

Colors that are seen by the eye or are visualized by the mind have an effect on the spiritual, even though the colors themselves are physical.

In the rest of Chapter 10, Cordovero discusses the different physical colors. He relates them to the different *Sefirot* and describes the relationship between meditating on a specific color and its corresponding *Sefira:*

> Thus if one wishes to bring down the Power of Mercy from the *Sefira* of *Chesed* (Mercy/Love), one should meditate on the color corresponding with this *Sefira* (White). One should focus on the color of the *Sefira* that is desired. If one wishes pure Mercy, then one meditates on pure white. If one desires less than pure mercy, one imagines a different white, a different kind of white, like the mortar of the ancient temple. . . . Similarly, if one wishes to do something through the transmission of judgment, then he should wear red vestments. He then visualizes the *Tetragrammaton*, seeing the Yod Hey Vav Hey in red letters.

Thus it is clear that when one wishes to involve the power of God in one's life, one uses the different colors of the different aspects of God, the *Sefirot*, and meditates on these colors by visualizing the יהוה (YHVH), the *Tetragrammaton*, in the appropriate colors.

Keter	No color or Extreme Whiteness
Chochmah	Sky Blue
Binah	Green (like grass)
Chesed	White & Silver
Gevurah	Blood Red & Antique Gold
Tiferet	Dark Purple
Netzach	Light Pink
Hod	Dark Pink
Yesod	A mixture of White shading to Orange-red and Orange-red shading to White. Also its color was sapphire-like, receiving all colors of the *Sefirot*.
Malchut	Royal Blue

Below is a table of the *Sefirot* and the different limbs and organs of the human body that they influence. This is a blueprint for helping you ascertain which *Sefira* and which color you should focus on as you prepare to practice the יהוה (YHVH). Finally, you focus on the יהוה (YHVH) in its twelve permutations with its specific color.

The Kabbalists over the ages have differed as to the specific relationship between a certain *Sefira* and its corresponding organ and limb. Nonetheless, they have encouraged us to meditate on the different parts of the human body using the *Sefirot* for wellness; just as the *Sefirot* help us to understand the unfolding nature of God, so do they help us to understand our own nature as we are created in the image of God.

The following table of the *Sefirot* and the different organs and limbs that they influence, based on teachings of the Kabbalists, works best for me in my prayers:

HEBREW NAME OF YHVH	COLOR	SEFIRA	ENGLISH TRANS. OF SEFIRA	ORGAN	LIMB
יהוה	Extreme Whiteness	Keter	Crown	Brain	N/A *A force of Divine Energy*
יהוה	Sky Blue	Chochmah	Wisdom	Lungs	Right side of head
יהוה	Grass green	Binah	Understanding	Heart	Left side of head
יהוה	White & Silver	Chesed	Compassion	Stomach	Right arm & shoulder
יהוה	Blood Red & Antique Gold	Gevurah	Judgment	Liver	Left arm and shoulder
יהוה	Dark Purple	Tiferet	Beauty	Gall bladder	Chest & back
יהוה	Light Pink	Netzach	Victory	Spleen	Right leg
יהוה	Dark Pink	Hod	Glory	Kidneys	Left leg
יהוה	White & Orange-red	Yesod	Foundation	Male genitals	Pelvis & rectal area
יהוה	Royal Blue	Malchut	Kingdom	Womb	Feet

Liberating Concept: יהוה YHVH works for everyone!

MELINDA   A woman approached me after a healing prayer class and said, "I don't think I can get into what you and the Rabbi are teaching but tell me more about this Paul Brunton fellow." I was delighted and directed her to healing meditations in volume seven of *The Notebooks of Paul Brunton*. They appear in the second chapter, titled "The Universal Life-Force."

These are universal principles. Paul Brunton studied with mystics and healers all over the world. The whole point is that each religion and tradition has its own rituals and one is not better than the other. Each person has to find a way that works with who they are. I am not a scholar of Paul Brunton nor of religion but, in my limited experience, every book I happened to pick up used the same language about the goal of connecting to something more than ourselves.

My cat, Rocky, thinks that she understands the world. Rocky looks and studies her surroundings with constant curiosity, but she has only a cat's brain. I have only a human brain, and it is also limited as I look out into the universe. If the world of subatomic particles can be true, then a God as a natural force in the universe can be true. I understand approximately the same amount about both and feel privileged to have caught a glimmer of something that is so much more than me.

The people who study subatomic physics say that the rules of Newtonian physics and Euclidean geometry do not apply at the subatomic level. Gary Zukav in his wonderful book, *The Dancing Wu Li Masters: An Overview of the New Physics*, calls this the mind-expanding discovery of quantum mechanics. It is a whole new way of looking at reality. In the subatomic realm, we cannot know both the position *and* the momentum of a particle with absolute precision. Zukav writes about the study of particles that are so tiny that "there are millions and millions of these subatomic particles in the smallest space that we can see." He says that "although Newton's physics could not account for phenomena in the microscopic realm, it continued to explain macroscopic phenomena very well (even though the macroscopic is made of the microscopic)! This was perhaps the most profound discovery of science."

Mysticism is another way of looking at reality. (For how mysticism and the new physics may actually be dealing with the same phenomena, see Zukav's chapter "The End of Science.") This is not a reality that we can "know" directly from our rational abilities or our senses but is a reality that we "know" from intuition. We get second-hand confirmation when we see and feel healing.

Rabbi Douglas and other mystics are saying that what we cannot understand with our limited rational ability, we can know through experiencing and intuition. Albert Einstein said, "The most beautiful thing we can express is the mysterious. . . .To know that what is impenetrable to us really exists, manifesting itself as the highest wisdom and the most radiant beauty which our dull faculties can comprehend only in their most primitive forms—this knowledge, this feeling, is at the center of true religiousness." He added, "In this sense, and in this sense only, I belong in the ranks of the devoutly religious men."

Use your curiosity and intuition to find what works for you. Even if you are skeptical, non-religious, or even anti-religious, suspend your disbelief long enough to try new techniques. Use your "beginner's mind." Judge from the experience and results if it "works" for you.

NEW TECHNIQUE: THE HEBREW LETTERS

Rabbi Douglas has always recommended that the prayer group use visualization of the Hebrew letters for the name of God or the word "God" in the Healing Prayer. During a difficult time for me, when someone I love dearly was in great pain, Rabbi Douglas asked if I would like to learn to use the Hebrew letters because he had found them to be so powerful in the Healing Prayer.

He quickly added that he would understand if I did not feel comfortable using Hebrew letters in my prayer because I am not Jewish. I remember smiling and saying to him that I did not care if it was a tradition from the most remote culture on Earth. It did not matter to me at all, as long as it helped me connect with God and bring about healing for this person I love so much.

I really do believe that God does not care which religion a person practices as long as one connects with God and is a good person. Though I also believe that other traditions and religions have healing practices equally as strong as the Hebrew letters, I had no access to them then. But, because of Rabbi Douglas, I do have access to what the Jewish mystics teach about the Hebrew letters and what an experience it is to use them! So, I experimented with the Hebrew letters.

I am not gifted at meditation (my mind still wanders quite a bit) or visualization (I am *just* beginning after four and a half years to be able to visualize). But when Rabbi Douglas taught me how to do the Healing Prayer using the Hebrew Letters, I began the same day. It was an astonishing experience. Using these letters added something to my prayer that I have never experienced before—the prayer was more joyful, intense and powerful! I felt a connection to God unlike anything I had ever experienced before.

The first day, he taught me how to do the permutations (visualizing the four Hebrew letters in different orders and moving them around during the prayer). Then the next week, he taught me to use the Hebrew letters with the different vowels.

My next step was to learn to visualize. From listening to prayer group members talk about visualization, it seems that some people naturally have the ability and some need to do exercises to learn to visualize. I needed to do the special "exercises" to gain this new skill. Visualization added a whole new dimension to the prayer. What fun it is to learn more and improve! My concentration increased a thousand-fold.

Rabbi Douglas taught me a common meditation exercise that he used when he began: Look at an object, or a picture (I used one of the Hebrew letters) for about thirty seconds, then close your eyes and concentrate on "seeing" it. Next, open your eyes and repeat the process over and over. Rabbi Douglas said that he would practice visualizing regularly for thirty minutes. My "exercising" lasted for ten minutes. I set a timer and even then had to almost force myself not to keep checking the time. This does not come naturally to me!

I made myself a simple chart and decided to practice visualizing for ten straight days. If I missed a day, I had to start over until I made it to ten in a row. This simple technique can be used for learning just about anything. After five days, I began to see the Yod! The image was faint, but every day after that I could see the letter a bit more clearly. After ten days, I could see the letter without using the paper. This success gave me so much incentive that I began to practice visualizing at various times during the day, and even when doing the Dream Angel Meditation at night.

My section of chapter seven deals with developing a plan. Begin simply. When you feel confident with one part of the prayer, add another. Practice, practice, practice. Each time I have added a new part, it has taken time and energy to make it a regular part of my life. After deciding to learn to visualize, it took me four months to work this extra ten minutes regularly into my daily practice.

Rabbi Douglas told me that during the prayer he visualizes himself swinging from the letters, going into the letters, jumping on the letters, dancing on the letters, bringing the letters into him. At our last prayer group meeting, he had the group visualize each letter shooting up into the sky. Try to substitute a new "activity" each day. It is essential to be creative and to do the prayer differently each time. Keep it new and make it your own.

Spontaneously, I began doing something during the prayer which the Rabbi does not do! What fun! During the part of the prayer: *The Lord is my strength,* I see myself running to the letters, embracing the letters, dancing with the letters, and jumping into the letters to fill me with Light. Each part of the Psalms becomes a different thing I do with each letter. For example, I visualize myself running to the Yod, then to the Hey, then to the Vav, then to the Hey. I feel the excitement and energy of the movement and connection with the letters. These feelings build inside of me as I visualize the light in me growing brighter and brighter.

Experiment with the prayer yourself. *Work* to discover what makes you feel joyful during the prayer. Faith, *kavvanah,* joy and novelty are the necessary ingredients! We are saying throughout this book: Experiment!! Have fun with this!! Find your own way.

Not long after learning to use the letters, I had a remarkable experience. My family went to Alaska to visit my brother, Tony, his lovely wife, Sally, and their girls, Maggie and Sara. We all hit the road together. Whether it was the trip or school starting again soon, a week before we left, my sixteen-year-old son, Jamey, developed an upset stomach that would not go away. He was nauseated all the time. In the airport, on the long flight, and after we got off the plane, he battled his stomach.

A day and a half later, both families took off for Denali National Park. We drove north from Anchorage, and Jamey was miserable the whole way. Four hours later we checked into our motel. Then we got up early the next morning and drove to the park.

Denali is a native word meaning "Great One," and that surely describes the magnificent mountain ranges and wildlife. We had reservations to ride in a bus along mountain roads without guard rails for *eleven hours*—five and a half hours in and five and a half hours out! Jamey was so sick and miserable that he could not stand still in line as we waited to board. I was beside myself: Should I make him go? Should he stay? Where would he stay? He would have to stay alone in a little motel room all day; I would stay with him, but there was no guarantee that he would not be sick anyway. He would miss Denali—the chance of a lifetime.

As is often the case with parenting, I did not know what to do. So, I started praying—and we all got on the bus. He put his head down and I continued to pray. I am sure that everyone on the bus thought that I was the sick one!

I closed my eyes, visualized the Light, saw the Hebrew letters in my mind, moved them around—in and out of me and in and out of Jamey, and said the Healing Prayer over and over. When I saw the Hebrew letters going into him, I could see him well. My concentration lasted only for a few seconds each time.

People on the bus kept calling out: caribou! moose! grizzly! eagle! wolf! And we would all jump up to look and take pictures. But I persevered. It took two hours. Suddenly, Jamey sat straight up, said, "This isn't so bad," smiled, and was absolutely fine for the rest of the day. At our next stop, he jumped off the bus and went running up a hill with his uncle and cousins. He was able to enjoy the rest of the vacation. We had a lovely time with our relatives and Alaska was astonishing.

I had desperately wanted my son to be well. Some people have told me that this was not the correct motivation for prayer: that one must accept God's will. I replied, How could it be God's will for my son to suffer? Rabbi Douglas taught me that God loves us so much that God's will is our will and our will is God's will. In a prayer group meeting Rabbi Douglas illustrated this with a reading from a Talmudic text, *Ethics of the Fathers*, which was written about two thousand years ago. The text reads, "Do His will as though it were thy will that He may carry out thy will as if it were His will." In other words, we say to God, "Let your will be my will and let my will be your will." Our wills are united. There is no separation. Rabbi Douglas and I are saying: Ask for what you want! Want something so badly—health, love, success, money, good things for those you love—that you are willing to work with and move God and access this force of Goodness! There is a partnership between God and us.

The YHVH was not a part of my life growing up, yet I have found it to be so powerful as part of my prayer. I like to think that the Jewish mystics discovered one way of seeing and experiencing the "fingertips" of God. My advice to you is to try it: You will only know if this is right for you if you try it and it works. There are no other criteria for success!

How to Do It

TWO MEDITATIONS FOR HEART FAILURE

RABBI DOUGLAS   The meditations in the first section of this chapter are powerful mystical calisthenics that bring us into the best state of mind for doing prayers for physical healing. The meditations in this section demonstrate how to apply what you have learned from doing them.

First meditation for heart failure

Here is a meditation for those who have suffered heart failure. This prayer can heal those cells damaged by heart attacks.

1. Find a place that you will use every day.

2. Sit down in a comfortable chair. Don't cross your legs or your arms. Be in relaxed clothing and unbuckle your belt.

3. Close your eyes and gently breathe in through your nostrils. Visualize your breath traveling from head to toe as you inhale. Then exhale through your mouth. Do this four times.

4. Either use the Candle Meditation or imagine that the whole room is filled with the light of God. Breathe in the light, not only through your nostrils, but through your whole body, until you see yourself and feel yourself filled with the light of God. Do this four times.

5. Meditate on the *Tetragrammaton*, focusing on the color of Binah, which is green like grass. Concentrate on the *Tetragrammaton*, with its twelve permutations, and visualize each of its permutations in this color green.

6. Visualize your physical heart and see the יהוה (YHVH) on your heart in green characters.

7. Repeat the following words, "Through the power of the Greater Mind, I pray that my circulatory system be in harmony within itself and with the other systems of my body. And with the Greater Mind, I visualize that my heart is bringing new life and vitality to cells of my body. And with the Greater Mind, I pray that no more damage be done to the cells of my heart. I pray that all cells damaged due to heart failure be made well."

8. Visualize yourself completely well and say, "Through the power of the Greater Mind, and through the Power of God, I am well." Visualize yourself completely well, doing some activity you did before the heart attack and say, "Thank you God for having healed me."

Second meditation for heart failure

Perhaps you wish to focus on the יהוה (YHVH) and its respective vocalizations for Binah, rather than on its color. Then, you would do the meditation as follows:

As in the previous meditation, sit in the comfortable chair you will use every day for the exercises, don't cross your arms or legs, be in relaxed clothing, unbuckle your belt, loosen your tie, etc.

1. Close your eyes and gently breathe in through your nostrils. Visualize your breath traveling from head to toe as you inhale. Then exhale through your mouth. Do this four times.

2. Either use the Candle Meditation or imagine that the whole room is filled with the light of God. Breathe in the light, not only through your nostrils, but through your whole body, until you see yourself and feel yourself filled with the light of God. Do this four times.

3. Instead of seeing יהוה (YHVH) with color, look at the vocalization for Binah (see p. 109), which is: YEY HEY VEY HEY. After you vocalize, YEY HEY VEY HEY, continue to vocalize all the different vocalizations of יהוה (YHVH), but focusing especially on the vocalization of YEY HEY VEY HEY.

4. Visualize your physical heart with the letters יְהֹוֶה (YEY HEY VEY HEY) superimposed on it.

5. Repeat the following words, "Through the power of the Greater Mind, I pray that my circulatory system be in harmony within itself and with the other systems of my body. And with the Greater Mind, I visualize that my heart is bringing new life and vitality to cells of my body. And with the Greater Mind, I pray that no more damage be done to the cells of my heart. I pray that all cells damaged due to heart failure be made well."

6. Visualize yourself completely well and say, "Through the power of the Greater Mind, and through the Power of God, I am well." Visualize yourself completely well, doing some activity you did before the heart attack and say, "Thank you God for having healed me."

9: OUR PRAYER GROUP

Universal Principle: The Power of Group Prayer

RABBI
DOUGLAS

THE JEWISH FAITH places great weight on the efficacy of group prayer. Indeed, the most important prayer the Jews pray is the *Amidah*. We pray this prayer three times daily. It consists of nineteen benedictions. This specific prayer is so important that another Hebrew term for the *Amidah* is *Ha-Tefilah*, which means "The Prayer."

Throughout the prayer, the individual members of the congregation use the first person plural pronoun, "We." So, when the individual is praying this private prayer, he does not pray to God to heal *him*, to prosper *him*, to deliver *him* from trouble. But, the individual worshipper, when invoking God, prays in the first person plural. So, for example, when he/she reaches the benediction or prayer for healing, he recites: "Heal us and we shall be healed. Help us and save us for You are our glory. Grant perfect healing for all our affliction."

For centuries, healing has been an integral part of the Jewish daily prayer service. It is Jewish custom to read the Torah on Mondays, Thursdays, and Saturday mornings; in Reform Jewish synagogues, we also read the Torah on Friday evenings. The Torah reading is divided into several parts, and a member of the congregation, or an honored guest, is usually given the honor of reciting the blessing before and after the Torah is read. This honor is called an *aliyah*. It is customary for the rabbi or prayer leader to recite a special healing prayer for someone who is ill, immediately after the honored guest prays the Torah blessing. This healing prayer is called the *Mi Shebeirach*. In some synagogues the *Mi Shebeirach* prayer is not said during the Torah service specifically; it can also be said during another part of the service.

In an Orthodox Jewish service today, as in ancient times, Jewish people are called to the *bima* (sacred area) by their Hebrew name and the Hebrew name of their father. (For example, I would be called David ben Gerson. My Hebrew name is David, and my father's Hebrew name was Gerson.) When a person's name is said for the *Mi Shebeirach* prayer, however, the ill person is called by his/her Hebrew name and his/her mother's name. (For example, I would be called David ben Shayna. My mother's Hebrew name is Shayna.)

Why? I think that it is in recognition of the mother's traditional role as caregiver, nurse, and nurturer. It appears to me that we use the mother's name in healing prayer to inspire in us an attachment to the feminine aspect of God. The traditional role of woman was the figure of compassion who nurtured her family as it grew and developed, whereas the male figure has always been seen as a warrior, a pursuer of justice.

Our tradition teaches that God created the world with the attribute of justice (*midat hadin*) and the attribute of compassion (*midat harachamim*). God's masculine and feminine aspects are both reflected in the creation story. Indeed, the Bible uses two words to define God in the first two chapters of Genesis. God is called *Elohim,* which means God of Justice, and God is called *Adonai,* which means God of Love. Whether it be Scripture or *Midrash,* our tradition encourages an understanding of the dichotomous nature of God, the masculine and the feminine. This is why I think that in asking us to recognize our mother's name in healing prayer, the early rabbis invited us to remember the feminine aspect of God in healing prayer.

Here is the traditional *Mi Shebeirach* prayer, taken from the *Rabbi's Manual:*

O God who blessed our ancestors Abraham, Isaac and Jacob, Sarah, Rebecca, Rachel and Leah, send your blessings to _____.[insert name of ill person], son/daughter of _____.[insert name of mother], have mercy on him/her and graciously restore his/her health and strength. Grant him/her a *refu-a sheleima,* complete recovery, along with all others who are stricken. May healing come speedily and let us say AMEN.

Our religion also teaches that when we pray for the healing of one person, we mention the names of others who are ill. We are all part of one community. We are all part of one *minyan,* composed of women and men.

We pray together as a group. Indeed, the Jewish religion maintains that many of our sacred prayers can *only* be said in a group, or in a *minyan.* A *minyan* is a community of ten persons. (According to Orthodox Judaism, they must be male and over thirteen years of age.)

The idea of *minyan* originated in the Biblical story of the Ten Spies. (Numbers 14:27) Moses sent twelve spies to search out the land of Canaan to verify its viability as the Jewish homeland. Ten spies lacked faith and advised against attempting to conquer the land. In the book of Numbers, these ten spies are referred to as an *edah.* The word *edah* means "congregation," and from this it has been deduced that a Jewish congregation for prayer must consist of at least ten adults— "ish" or "Adam" in Orthodoxy.

In Orthodox Judaism, the Hebrew word "ish" or "Adam" is translated as "man." Even though the translation of these words as "man" is accurate in many Biblical and rabbinic narratives, we can also translate this word to mean "people." Non-Orthodox Judaism comfortably accepts this philological approach.

Also, historical imperatives demanded the Orthodox translation, but in contemporary times, we recognize the sanctity of woman. This is not only because she also was created in the image of God, but because the God to whom we pray—has both a masculine (*Hakadosh Barukh Hu*) and a feminine (*Shekhina*) aspect.

Every other Wednesday, our prayer group meets together, sharing our hopes and our visions for healing. The group consists of Christians and Jews, most of whom are fighting different serious diseases. We pray for one another, using the healing meditations explained in this book. And in our prayer, we hope to bring down the spirit of God upon each and every one of us, and to influence God to offer us healing.

An amazing mystical text in the *Zohar* illustrates what we try to do in our prayer group. I translate it as follows.

> Rabbi Eliezer began a commentary on the verse, "Why, when I came was no one there? Why, when I called, would none respond?" [Isaiah 50:2] How beloved is Israel before the Holy One Praised be He? Because wherever they dwell, the Holy One Praised be He is found among them. Because He never removes from them His love, just as it is written, "And let them make Me a Sanctuary that I may dwell among them." [Exodus 25:8] . . . "That they make Me a Sanctuary . . ." any sanctuary, because every synagogue in this world is called a sanctuary. And already they established it. And the *Shekhina* precedes the worshippers to the synagogue.
>
> Each person who is among the first ten to enter the synagogue is praised since together they [the quorum of ten, the *minyan*] form something complete. And they are the first to be satisfied by the *Shekhina*.
>
> And already we have learned that it is necessary that the ten persons should come together at the same time and they should not come separately, so as not to delay the completion of the members of the body [since all ten are like members of one body among whom God dwells]. Because the Holy One, blessed be He, created man whole in one act and created him with all his bodily members together. "Is not He the Father who created you, fashioned you and made you endure?" [Deuteronomy 32:6]
>
> Come and see, just as all the members of Adam were completed at the same time [by God], each member having a function; therefore, when the *Shekhina* comes early into the synagogue, it is necessary that ten people be found there as one and the desired perfection be attained [because a true congregation has ten people for they correspond to the ten *Sefirot*—there is always ten]. Afterwards, every thing can be restored. And how do we effect this complete restoration? In accordance with what is written in the Biblical verse, "A numerous people is the glory of the King."

[Proverbs 14:28] And according to this the people who come afterwards restore the body.

We learn from this Kabbalistic text that God is present when there is a quorum of ten people, teaching us that the Presence of God is strengthened when we pray in a community. The Kabbalistic text also teaches that these ten symbolize the ten *Sefirot*—that is, the ten aspects of the one God. And so, it is not only important that there be ten in prayer, it is also important to be among the first ten who enter the sanctuary. This indicates that you are part of God, and God is part of you. This is one way, and an honor, to become filled with the Presence of God. We then read in the text that the ten should come at the same time, since the *minyan* represents the Sefirotic realm, and all the *Sefirot* together make up the Presence of God. Since God is not divided up into small parts, but is one unity, so should the *minyan* be like God. The mystical idea of *minyan* is more than a group of people coming together in prayer. Rather, it is the Presence of God right here on earth. Hence, to be part of the *minyan* of the original ten is to be part of God.

This Kabbalistic interpretation that the original ten have a mystical nature about them is further explained as we continue to read the Kabbalistic text of the *Zohar*, Parashat Naso:

> But when the *Shekhina* precedes the ten men of the quorum, that is: the ten men did not come together as they should have, the Holy One blessed be He shouts: "Why do I come and there is no man?" What does "And there is no man" mean? It means that the members of the body have not been restored, so the body is not completed (the members of the body representing the individual members of the congregation and the body representing the congregation per se), because when the body is not complete, "there is no man" (no complete harmony among the ten *Sefirot*).
>
> And because of this, (it is precisely stated "and there is no man.") Come and see when the body is complete below (when the *minyan* is complete), a celestial holiness (the holiness of the ten *Sefirot* of God) comes and enters this body (*minyan*) and the

minyan becomes a real representation of the ten *Sefirot*. So, every-one must be careful not to talk of profane matters, since Israel is then in a state of heavenly perfection, and is sanctified through a celestial sanctity. They are great.

We learn here that the *minyan* can be the embodiment of God, because the *Shekhina* enters the *minyan*. This feminine aspect of God that enters the *minyan* allows Israel and the masculine aspect of God to touch. So, this world in which we live becomes a replica of the heav-enly world when we have a proper *minyan*. Furthermore, the ten *Sefirot* working in complete harmony with one another are internalized by the first ten of the *minyan*.

Our Wednesday night *minyan* is composed of men and women, and it has the potential to be holy. The first ten who arrive bring a super-nal sanctity to the larger group. I feel that this spiritual energy has allowed members of our community *minyan* to feel spiritual healing.

The emphasis in Judaism is not on individual private prayer, but on group prayer. But a good part of my ministry is also praying with people privately. Healing prayer does not *mandate* a prayer group, but the Judeo-Christian tradition feels that group prayer *adds* to the effi-cacy and power of individual prayer. That's why I often suggest to people with whom I pray privately on a regular basis, that they form their own prayer group in their homes to practice the same prayers that we outline in this book. I suggest that these people invite to their group people who love them dearly and people whom they love very much, to create a strong atmosphere of love in the room. It is also important, of course, to have people who have faith. This combination of love and faith is dynamite.

At these prayer groups, it is best to do the Healing Prayer that we outlined in chapter five. Before the group meets for Healing Prayer, it is wise if the individual participants study the Healing Prayer before-hand and also study how to be in the Greater Mind. Prayer is an art, and it requires practice. A person who practices prayer is more adept at prayer than a person who doesn't practice prayer. Just as you have to practice the violin or golf or oil painting before you become highly skilled in those fields, the same is so with prayer. You should practice and practice these meditations so that your skill will develop and you will become an expert "pray-er."

Also, when you enter a prayer group, bringing in the Presence of God, your actions in the world count a lot! You can't be a loving "pray-er" for one hour and be a nasty person the rest of the day. You may think you are praying with love and faith, but if your physical actions reflect the opposite, your group prayer will be ineffective. Your life should testify to the fact that you really do believe that every person is made in the image of God. This means that you should regularly share your money in charitable donations and in gifts to people who are homeless.

When you do this, you are exercising your soul. And when your soul develops spiritual muscle, your prayers and your ability to connect with God are substantially stronger than if your soul is "flabby." Inherent in a well-developed soul is a strong faith that God can do and will do, plus love for people—especially, love for the person you are praying for—and for yourself.

Jennifer, a young married woman in my community, the mother of two daughters, was diagnosed two years ago with metastatic breast cancer after undergoing a lumpectomy the year before. The bone marrow stopped functioning normally. She was not producing the red and white blood cells she needed to live. Jennifer was very scared. She found wonderful physicians at the University of Chicago, who were treating her very well with chemotherapy. But I also suggested that we pray together.

When people come to see me privately, I usually pray with them and with people they love in front of the open Ark. But in this instance, Jennifer was too ill and weak in the beginning to drive to the synagogue. So, my wife Peggy and I drove to her home to pray with her every week. We prayed in her home, in her bedroom, which was the most relaxing room for her. And every week, there was always a group of people present to join in the prayer sessions—her husband, her mother and stepfather, her sisters, her cousin, and her friends. These people loved Jennifer, and they studied the Healing Prayer beforehand.

These people prayed with faith. After a few months, Jennifer was well enough to meet me at the synagogue where we continued our regular weekly prayer. After her chemotherapy and months of regular prayer, her doctors have been amazed at her recovery.

As Jennifer says, "After the chemotherapy, I began my recovery slowly. At first I could barely walk to the end of the driveway and back. But slowly, to my doctors' astonishment, my blood counts began to rise. It is almost two years now since my last chemotherapy treatment, and my counts are virtually normal. I now walk two miles a day. Not a day goes by without my becoming overwhelmed with gratitude. I see my doctor every three months, but I still pray daily. Healing is not something that happens and is over, not with cancer. Healing is a daily necessity, and prayer is healing."

Even though the *minyan* and group prayer, when done with the proper *kavvanah* (dedication) and the proper *kevah* (technique) afford wonderful results, private prayer at times can be electrifying. It is during private prayer that I am able to get into an ecstatic state. In this state, my whole being is focused on the Presence of God. In *minyan* prayer, I think we are more sensitive to other people around us, and I have seen that most people are more restrained. So I understand why, at times, people would prefer to do private prayer for their spouses, or an aunt, or loved one who is ill. My suggestion is that you do both.

Doing both kinds of prayer regularly, for yourself or your wife or your aunt, takes a lot of time. But isn't your loved one worth it? There is nothing more precious to you than the life and health of your partner. Your aunt helped your mom raise you and if you want God to heal you, you must work hard, very hard, at prayer—inviting God, struggling with God, even fighting with God so that you and God become one and you become healed.

At Congregation Bene Shalom, we offer healing prayer during our weekday morning *minyan,* or during our Sabbath services (Friday night/Saturday morning). The prayer is said in our synagogue just before we say the *Amidah* or Silent Prayer. I and the congregation visualize the person we are praying for. We visualize him or her well, knowing with faith that God's healing has already begun as soon as we utter the prayer.

During the week, people from our community call the temple office and ask that certain names be added to the prayer list. For example, one woman regularly asks us to put down the names of her three daughters, even though these young ladies and their mother never come to Sabbath services to pray for themselves. The mother believes, as do many others, that if somehow the rabbi were to call on God to heal these people, they would be miraculously healed. And even though I have preached sermons and taught classes that good prayer is work, involving visualization and faith and practice, some people of our congregation still believe that they themselves don't have to participate in this prayer practice.

The rabbi is not the High Priest who says your prayer for you. As a matter of fact, Judaism teaches that we are a kingdom of priests. Each one of us is a priest; each one of us is a priest directing our prayers to God, without intermediary. Each individual has the right and the privilege to learn how to pray, and to do these prayers for her children.

This is not to say that I don't pray for individual members of our community. I definitely do. And these prayers are strong. But, I also ask that the person for whom I am praying also pray for him- or herself—or at the very least, that a loved one be involved in learning how to pray for this person on a regular basis.

If we want God to be involved in our lives, enter our lives and bring us healing, we personally must testify to the greatness of God. Isaiah says it best, "So you are my witnesses declares the Lord, and I am God." (Isaiah 43:12) This means that when you testify to God's healing power, you make God real and active. You witness to God. When you don't testify to God's healing power and greatness, you are not witnessing to God. We and God are partners. We work together, making this world a great place. The Judeo-Christian tradition teaches that God created the world, but it is humanity's responsibility to finish the task. And furthermore, after God had created the moon, the sun, the stars, the sky, the beasts, the birds and the fish, God decided to create woman and man. The angels protested that if God created human beings, there would be war and bloodshed. But God did create human beings, our tradition teaches, so that there would be someone here on earth to testify to God's greatness.

Liberating Concept: Group prayer— the whole is worth more than the sum of its parts!

MELINDA   Working in the field of deafness, having deaf friends, and having a deaf foster daughter has allowed me the privilege of meeting the nicest people, deaf and hearing. Deafness, which can isolate people, can also bring people together in marvelous ways.

Recently I attended a Catholic Mass and ceremony celebrating the fifteenth birthday of the daughter of my friends, Bertha and Rogelio Ramos. Their hearing daughter, Maria, signed a Gospel reading and spoke in Spanish. Her deaf brother, Rogelio, signed another reading. Father Joseph Mulcrone—a remarkably talented and Godly man—said the Mass in English, Spanish, and American Sign Language. Walking into the church, I met two deaf children and their hearing parents; by the end of the evening, we were much more than acquaintances. When I said goodbye to the mother, she smiled and said that she knew we would meet again at a "deaf" function. The Deaf World is like that.

Experiences like this happen every day at Congregation Bene Shalom. Our prayer group has deaf and hearing members with a sign language interpreter. Congregation Bene Shalom is the most inclusive place I have ever been. Rabbi Douglas brings people together. Our prayer group has deaf and hearing people, Jews and Christians of many denominations, Catholics, Quakers, a member of the Baha'i faith, and people with no formal religious affiliation. *This is for everyone.* We see this every time we meet.

When we are together on Wednesday nights, we are all moved to experience God as a powerful energy or force that transcends religious denominations. It is absolutely breathtaking to look around the room filled with so many differences and be part of such an experience that makes us all the same. What a contrast to the world history my son studied last year. Jamey and I finally condensed world history into: "Which religion is persecuting and killing which other religion in which country?" What a truly magnificent opportunity we have been given to pray together!

As Rabbi Douglas says, we encourage people to bring a close family member or friend to the group—someone who will be their "prayer partner" on a daily basis. Love is a powerful and essential ingredient for the Healing Prayer.

One Jewish member of the prayer group has a Catholic prayer partner. We have a Jewish woman in our group who was brought up with nuns and then was the cantorial soloist at Bene Shalom for many years. We have a deaf man who joined Bene Shalom as a teenager. In one couple, the wife is Jewish and her husband is Christian. They both come together to worship God—not the God of the Hebrews or Christians or Buddhists or Muslims but the God of all people. We come together from many religions and many walks of life. There are young and old, deaf and hearing, an M.D., a Ph.D. in nursing, graduate students, student rabbis, a delivery man, homemakers, psychotherapists, business people, teachers, and a school principal.

This group grew out of a class that Rabbi Douglas and I had taught on Healing Prayer. After two years of teaching, many of the students said, "We now know how to pray. Let's do it. Let's have a prayer group." The only requirement for the group is that one wants to pray. Each member is devoted to their own faith yet each of us also recognizes that there is a higher faith than our own ecclesiastical community. This is the faith in the universal power of God.

We come together in a higher faith and in a Greater Mind, and we share an experience that is emotionally sustaining for all of us.

Human beings need healthy relationships in order to survive and grow. Emotional sustenance, empathic resonance, and psychological oxygen are the lovely metaphors Heinz Kohut uses in his classic book, *How Does Analysis Cure?*. He said that the "experience of the availability of empathic resonance" from healthy others is "the major constituent of the sense of security in adult life."

We are social creatures and relationships are what this life is all about. The Ba'al Shem Tov said that offering joy to others is a very great thing. To use his images, it is a very great thing to walk into a place where people smile at you, ask you how you are doing, and say nice things to you. It feels wonderful to be so cared about and valued. The group gives all of us psychological/emotional oxygen.

In this group we have also experienced the power of what can happen when people pray together. Jesus said, "Where two or three are gathered in my name, I am there among them." (Matthew 18:20). He was describing the power of group prayer to bring God in. This is a universal spiritual law or principle. The whole is indeed worth more than the sum of its parts. God is a spiritual force in the universe and, like a physical force, acts out of necessity. God is governed by spiritual laws that are just as natural as the law of gravity. If you throw a ball up, it necessarily comes down. Similarly, if one prays in the Greater Mind, God necessarily responds. This is also behind the mystical concept of *minyan*. Rabbi Douglas taught us that when we pray together, God cannot help but become a participant because we ignite the Presence of God that lives within the group. God cannot act alone but needs us as partners.

This is a different concept of God. This God is a force of goodness and compassion in the universe that we can learn to work with.

People often say to me, how can you believe in God when a truly terrible thing happens? I can only reply that I believe in a God that is a force for good in the universe that needs us to help create more good. These techniques to access this God have forever changed my life. This is so much more than I ever expected. What an incredible gift!

Albert Einstein said,

> In our endeavor to understand reality we are somewhat like a man trying to understand the mechanism of a closed watch. He sees the face and the moving hands, even hears its ticking, but he has no way of opening the case. If he is ingenious he may form some picture of a mechanism which could be responsible for all the things he observes, but he may never be quite sure his picture is the only one which could explain his observations. He will never

be able to compare his picture with the real mechanism and he cannot even imagine the possibility of the meaning of such a comparison.

To me, God is the closed watch. I know the Healing Prayer works but I may never understand how it works. I may never know what is inside of the "clock." But I have seen, heard, touched, and experienced physical healing. Seeing is believing. If you are willing to suspend disbelief, then see for yourself!

Every week in the prayer group, people ask Rabbi Douglas questions. He loves questions. He always begins his answers with "in my experience." He means that no one tradition is better than another. He is teaching us what he has learned from years of study and practice.

In one prayer group meeting, a deaf man, Barry Levine, asked an important question. He asked if a deaf person can pray as well as a hearing person, even though some deaf people do not choose to speak. He wanted to know if deafness would limit a person's ability to practice the Healing Prayer. Rabbi Douglas answered that deafness is no hindrance. In fact, deafness can heighten a person's reliance on intuition and this is a benefit to the prayer and to the experience of God. The whole point is that, during prayer, we do not focus on what our senses tell us. We focus on our inner experience, our intuition.

Rabbi Douglas and I are currently writing a book that includes a deaf philosopher who lived in Baghdad *circa* 1100 CE. His name was Abu'l Barakat and he served in the Sultan's court as a physician. At that prayer meeting, Rabbi Douglas spoke of this deaf philosopher. He was born a Jew but later converted to Islam when he feared for his life. He struggled the remainder of his years with his conversion.

What made Barakat unique and valuable was that he had the experience of being first a hearing man and later a deaf man. After becoming deaf, he could no longer practice medicine and turned to meditation and philosophy. He came to attach greater importance to intuitive truth than the established Greek rational truth of Aristotle's philosophy, which equates truth with what is seen and heard.

Barakat, confronted with his own deafness, insisted that we need not look outside ourselves to discover truth. He realized that truth does not need to be discovered by reason and sense experience; truth is discovered by intuition and inner experience. He created a bold theory of self-awareness which reduces the ear and eye to merely physical instruments while exalting the soul as the repository of all auditive and visual forms. It is the soul that hears.

Barakat's deafness taught him that he is not aware of God's existence through the use of his senses, but his awareness of God is gained through intuitive knowledge. This is exactly what we teach. The knowledge of God, the experience of God, the unification with God, comes about through intuition. God is within you, and finding this God makes Him/Her your partner. The deaf philosopher, Abu'l Barakat, teaches us to listen more carefully inside ourselves.

The power of the prayer group is growing as we all learn to focus and become better "pray-ers." However, the group is only a part of the process. One must pray for oneself and others every day in order for successful healing to take place. An example of this is Barry Levine, the thirty-nine-year-old deaf man who comes to the prayer group regularly and prays for himself twice every day. He wrote of his experience:

> My name is Barry Levine and I have known Rabbi Douglas since I was a teenager. I began praying with the rabbi for healing when I moved back to Chicago in 1997. I am HIV positive. The rabbi and healing are amazing. I already have part of a miracle inside of me because of the prayer and medicine working together. I feel great in the prayer group when everyone prays for me and I like to pray for everyone else. The prayer helps me continue to stay healthy. When I pray with the rabbi, it is a very great thrill, getting closer to God. I pray by myself every morning and every night. I have many plans for the future. I am working part time now and hope to go back to school in the spring. I will go to Las Vegas for a long vacation.

In the prayer group, we come together regularly to pray for each other. We cannot pray for everyone each week since there are many of us. The Healing Prayer requires energy and concentration. It takes great work to share the Light of God with those we love. So, even if we have forty people in the group, we will only pray for seven. It is wonderful that the thirty-three generously share God's healing. Of course, when you give, you get. Everyone leaves the prayer group with a heightened sense of God.

Among the impediments to prayer, especially in a group, are all of the foreign thoughts that bombard us: "I forgot to wash the gym uniforms! Are my children doing their homework right now? Will my business deal succeed?" The last part of this chapter gives a wonderful meditation to strengthen our concentration (our spiritual muscles!) so that when we begin praying as a group, we are all focused on God.

How to Do It

Preparing for group prayer

RABBI DOUGLAS   Here is a meditation based on the teachings of the laws relative to the *Amidah*, in the *Shulkhan Aruch*, Section *Orach Chayyim*. This text teaches that when you pray, you should focus on the prayers to such an extent that you banish from your mind all thoughts that trouble you. When you pray, it's necessary that you speak your prayers with great preparation. You should feel as though you are speaking to a mortal king; consequently you should prepare your speech and give all respect to that king. How much the more should you stand in awe when you pray, since you are speaking not to a mortal king but to the King of the universe? You speak as if the *Shekhina* is facing you, removing all troubling thoughts that remain with you. You don't even think lewd thoughts because you know that God understands and reads the thoughts of all people.

Here is a meditation that each person should do before embarking on a group prayer:

1. Imagine you are sitting, facing a throne. On this throne is a powerful light and this powerful light is the *Shekhina*, or Immanent Presence of God. Try to feel this Light and bring this Light within you so that you become one with God's Presence.

2. Remove from your thoughts and your mind all troubling or inter-
fering thoughts. Think only of the Presence that is before you and
that you are bringing within you.

To facilitate this, breathe in the light gently, inhaling and exhal-
ing so that shortly, you feel as though God is not only outside, but
inside of you. If a troubling thought occurs to you, banish that
thought immediately, so that all these thoughts are completely nul-
lified. When you feel that the Lord God has entered you and is
before you, that you are in the Presence of God and also practicing
the Presence of God, and you feel the sense of awe and trepidation
and honor, you are ready to participate honestly in group prayer.

After you do this meditation, then you are filled with the Presence of
God, and able and prepared to do healing prayers with the group. All
of the meditations and prayers given in this book are appropriate for
group prayer.

EPILOGUE

RABBI
DOUGLAS   I REMEMBER the day I met Rabbi Dresher. I was walking with a cane and was told by my orthopedic surgeon that the probability of amputating my left leg was great. I went to Rabbi Dresher, unsure if he could teach me how to embrace God and receive healing. But, I knew I didn't want to lose my left leg.

I remember entering his West Rogers Park apartment. I was awed by his library of books, but I was inspired by his warm smile, his learning and his great patience and compassion in teaching me.

He never charged me for my regular weekly visits. I was also moved because, even though I was a Reform rabbi, and he was an Orthodox rabbi, he treated me as a brother in faith. He was such a kind person.

I am sad that Rabbi Dresher died several years ago at the age of ninety-one. He is not here to see his teachings reach fruition in this book. Because of his greatness and his knowledge of mysticism, he allowed me to understand the word of God as taught by Moses when he lectured before the ancient Israelites, as they studied in the desert:

> Surely the teaching which I teach you is not too complicated for you. Nor is it beyond reach. It is not in the heavens that you should say "Who among us can go up to the heavens and get it for us and teach it to us that we may do it?" Neither is it beyond the sea, that you should say, "Who among us can cross to the other side of the sea and get it for us and teach it to us that we may do it?" Know God is very close to you, in your mouth and in your heart, to worship Him. (Deuteronomy 30:11–14)

Detail from *The Healer*, 1998, by
Rabbi Douglas Goldhamer

APPENDIX:
EMOTIONAL HEALING AND JOY

MELINDA One indicator of emotional health is the capacity to experience joy. There are many roads to joy. In this appendix, I call special attention to skills, services, books, and other resources that have been enormously helpful to me and others I have worked with.

1. Practicing the Art of Prayer

Doing the prayer and seeing the healing brings me faith and joy. Practicing the Healing Prayer and meditations contributes to emotional health and emotional health contributes to the efficacy of the Healing Prayer and meditations. It is a positive cycle.

2. Psychotherapy

Psychotherapy and self-help can be very effective for many emotional difficulties. The best book I have ever read about the process of psychotherapy is:

Between Therapist and Client: The New Relationship by Michael Kahn. Dr. Kahn highlights the contributions of Heinz Kohut, the founder of Self Psychology.

3. Treatment for Neurobiological Disorders

Research consistently shows that psychotherapy in conjunction with medication for neurobiological disorders is the most effective means of treatment for most people with these disorders (for most, not for all). Many factors come into play with neurobiological disorders including genetics, prenatal history, and trauma, both in childhood and adulthood.

Books and articles I have found most helpful in this area include: *You Mean I Don't Have to Feel This Way? New Help for Depression, Anxiety, and Addiction,* by Charlotte Dowling. This book offers an excellent discussion of neurobiological disorders, including depression, bulimia, panic disorders, phobias, some forms of binge eating, ADHD, hair pulling, kleptomania, and gambling addiction. These disorders have all responded to treatment with various medications that target specific neurotransmitters in the brain.

"Panic Pathway: Study of Fear Shows Emotions Can Alter 'Wiring' of the Brain" from *The New Times*, by Michael Waldholz. Neurobiological disorders are affected by both heredity and by life experience. There is increasing evidence that childhood trauma can cause changes in brain function. Research at Yale University has shown that fear can alter the "wiring" of the brain. Scientists believe that "nerve circuits recently found to contain and convey powerful memories are deeply seared by a frightening ordeal." (p. A6)

Brain Lock: Free Yourself from Obsessive-Compulsive Behavior by Jeffrey Schwartz, M.D. Within weeks of being given medication, many with obsessive compulsive disorder, OCD, are able to stop compulsively washing their hands, counting, checking, and having repetitive, intrusive thoughts. OCD is not the result of intrapsychic conflict or of faulty parenting. OCD has a strong hereditary component. In addition, scientists at UCLA have found what they call a "brain lock" on the right side of the brain. Using PET scans (positron emission tomography) clearly demonstrates that the orbital cortex, the underside of the front of the brain, is hypermetabolic, or overheated, in people with OCD. (p. 48)

Taking Charge of ADHD: The Complete, Authoritative Guide for Parents, by Russell Barkley, Ph.D. Children and adults with ADHD "just can't get it together." The varied symptoms are caused by brain function and the diagnosis is often missed. As a psychotherapist, I listen for: can't sit still, doesn't pay attention, disruptive, unorganized, forgetful, "spacey," difficulty in planning for the future, constantly seeking stimulation, poor social skills, lag in achievement, oppositionality, and seeks attention with misbehavior. With adults, there is often an addiction or addictive behavior and terrible management of money. These symptoms wreak havoc on self-esteem and on relationships. Poor parenting does not cause these problems. This is an excellent book.

Driven to Distraction: Recognizing and Coping with Attention Deficit Disorder from Childhood through Adulthood, by Edward Hallowell, M.D. and John Ratey, M.D. In the preface, Dr. Hallowell writes movingly about realizing that he himself had ADD. Hallowell's reaction was, "I felt as if a boulder had been lifted from my back. I wasn't all the names I'd been called in grade school— "a daydreamer," "lazy," "an under-achiever," "a spaceshot" —and I didn't have some repressed unconscious conflict that made me impatient and action-oriented." (pp. ix, x) The most damaging effect of ADD and ADHD is the repeated experience of failure and criticism without knowing the reason!

"A.D.D. WareHouse." 300 Northwest 70TH Avenue, Suite 102, Plantation, FL 33317. The A.D.D. WareHouse is a catalogue that is described as the leading resource for the understanding and treatment of Attention Deficit Disorders and related problems. To request a copy of this catalog, call 1-800-792-8944.

4. Learning to Think, Feel, and Act Differently

Paul Brunton said, "There is only room in your mind for a single thought at a time. Take care, then, that it be a positive one." (*Perspectives*, p. 155) What a task for us humans! I had to *learn* to think and act positively! Books and articles I have found most helpful include:

Women and Risk: How to Master Your Fears and Do What You Never Thought You Could Do, by Nicky Marone. This is another wonderful book for men and women, old and young. It is full of help for learning to overcome patterns of behavior learned in childhood. Ms. Marone writes about two styles of meeting challenges: mastery-oriented and learned helplessness. Mastery-oriented people see the inevitable difficulties in learning new things as external factors that can be changed. Those with learned helplessness tend to see themselves negatively and not take risks. They see obstacles and problems as stemming from their own personal deficiencies—not being smart or talented enough, etc.—instead of just an inherent part of learning something new.

"Parents Can Help Girls Win Confidence Game," *The Chicago Tribune*, by Melinda Stengel. Girls and women can learn to enjoy being assertive and competitive. We can change our identities to include enjoyment of our own personal power.

Awaken the Giant Within: How to take immediate control of your mental, emotional, physical & financial destiny, by Anthony Robbins. This is a truly remarkable book. Robbins writes about how to "constantly improve your ability to enjoy your life." (p. 97) He uses the same language about learning to think positively that Rabbi Douglas, Agnes Sanford, Paul Brunton, and many others use. Robbins has the best method I have ever come across for changing how one is feeling at any moment (in chapter 11) and for changing what he calls "limiting patterns" of behavior (in chapter 6).

The Healing Light, by Agnes Sanford. Mrs. Sanford offers similar techniques for overcoming negativity! She writes: "the part of us that reasons is only one-tenth of the consciousness. Psychologists tell us that nine-tenths of our thoughts lie below the level of consciousness. Moreover, it is this submerged part of the consciousness—this subconscious mind—that controls our bodies. . . We ignore the old thought-habit . . . We must also gently and patiently teach ourselves a new thought-habit. We must re-educate the subconscious mind, replacing every thought of fear with a thought of faith, every thought of illness with a thought of health, every thought of death with a thought of life. In other words, we must learn faith." (pp. 30, 33)

Open Mind, Open Heart: The Contemplative Dimension of the Gospel, by Thomas Keating. Father Keating is a Cistercian priest, monk, and abbot who lives in a Benedictine monastery. This book teaches centering and contemplative prayer that has as its goal the development and deepening of the relationship with God. He writes that this type of prayer is open to everyone: "you only have to be a human being to be eligible to become a contemplative." (p. 41) His techniques for meditation are the best I have ever read. He also writes about using this type of prayer to restructure the nervous system and psyche (p. 98)— in other words, for emotional healing.

NOTES

Chapter 1: God is a Force in the Universe and in Us

1. A *mezuzah* literally means "doorpost" because it is attached to the doorpost of every Jewish home, symbolizing the Jew's loyalty to God, loyalty to the Jewish people. Many also see the *mezuzah* as a source of divine protection. The *mezuzah* consists of a small case containing a piece of parchment with two Biblical passages (Deuteronomy 6:4-9 and 11:13-31) which includes the *Shema* prayer.

2. The Zoharic Passage from which the Candle Meditation derives is: "We may say that he who desires to penetrate to the mystery of the holy unity should contemplate the flame which rises from a burning coal or candle." (Rabbi Simeon bar Yochai, *Sefer Ha-Zohar,* with Sulam Commentary, translated by Harry Sperling and Maurice Simon, part I, pp. 50b-51a.)

Chapter 2: Learning Faith

1. The Hebrew word *Adonai* is the name of God that symbolizes the God of love. Another Hebrew name for God is *Elohim,* which represents "God as a God of justice." These two names: *Adonai* and *Elohim* are used throughout Biblical literature and in the liturgy of the Jewish people. In this prayer, we are petitioning the God of Love, *Adonai,* to inspire our Dream Angel to visit us.

Chapter 3: The Greater Mind

1. The *Midrash* is composed of numerous books of Biblical exegesis by Jewish authorities in the ancient era. These homiletical commentaries are filled with parables, allegories and colorful narratives.

2. As Aryeh Kaplan says in his book, *Jewish Meditation: A Practical Guide* (p. 13), "One of the most powerful uses of meditation is to gain an awareness of the spiritual. . . . if a person can quiet down all extraneous thought, he can then 'tune in' to the spiritual. This tuning-in is what is known as the mystical experience. In this sense, meditation is the most important technique of mystics all over the world."

Chapter 6: The Commandment to Rejoice

1. Born in Israel in 1542, Chaim Vital was among the most important influences of later Kabbalah. He was a major disciple of Isaac Luria (see note 2, below). Following Luria's death in 1572, Vital compiled Luria's teachings in writing and offered his own interpretation of these teachings. Vital's extensive writings were compiled in such works as *Etz Ha-Hayyim* and *Etz Ha-Da'at*. One of these books, *Etz Ha-Hayyim*, includes all the teachings of Isaac Luria through Chaim Vital's perspective. One of the texts within *Etz Ha-Hayyim* is *Sha'arei Kedushah*, which was first published in Constantinople in 1734.

2. Isaac Luria was a Palestinian Jewish mystic living in Palestine during the sixteenth century. He is also called *Ha-Ari* (The Lion). Isaac Luria was greatly influenced by another great Kabbalist, Moses Cordovero, who also lived in Palestine at that time. Isaac Luria attracted a circle of devotees and mystical followers. Their community was in the holy city of Safed. He practiced with his mystical followers prayers involving the *Sefirot* and prayers and meditations combining the letters of the Divine Names. Luria's meditations were called *kavvanot*. His teachings were collected and compiled by Chaim Vital, in the text *Etz Ha-Hayyim*.

Chapter 8: Alternative Meditations

1. The three most holy books of the Jewish tradition are the Bible, Talmud, and *Zohar*. The *Zohar* is the most important book of our mystical literature. (The Kabbalah is the body of literature that comprises Jewish mystical teaching. The *Zohar* is one of the many

books of the Kabbalah.) Many religious people believe that the *Zohar* was the work of an early Talmudic scholar, Rabbi Simeon bar Yochai. However, modern scholars believe it is the major work of a thirteenth-century Spanish scholar, Moses de Leon. The *Zohar* was written as a mystical commentary to the Torah, as well as on other books of the Hebrew Bible. The *Zohar* opens to us the esoteric and hidden meaning of God's Torah. For example, even though the Torah does not speak of the *Sefirot*, this is a key teaching of the *Zohar*. The *Zohar* maintains that God made man in the manlike image of the *Sefirot*—the Ten Powers that unfold from God as He creates the Universe. This manlike image of the *Sefirot* is called Adam Kadmon, or Supernal Man.

2. The oldest Hebrew word for "prayer" is found in the Bible. The word is *avodah*, which also means "work." Prayer was, and is, work. If you are not working, you are not praying. If it doesn't hurt, you are not praying. The modern Hebrew word for "prayer" is *liheat-palel*, which means "to verbally struggle." When you pray, you struggle. If we want to reach God, we have to work and struggle.

3. The names of the *Sefirot* are believed to be borrowed from the following verse in I Chronicles 29:11, "Thine O Lord is the greatness, and the power, and the glory, and the victory, and the majesty: for all that is in heaven and on earth is thine; thine is the kingdom, O Lord, and Thou art exalted as head above all."

4. It is with the *Sefirot* that God creates the Universe. All created things came into being through the *Sefirot*. God created the world by allowing the ten *Sefirot* to emanate or unfold from Him.

As we have already seen, God expresses Himself in the emanation of the *Sefirot*. Though God is greater than the totality of the *Sefirot*, God works through the *Sefirot* by means of which He passes from unity to plurality. The initial purpose of the Kabbalistic Sefirotic system was to explain intermediaries between God and this world of ours, to bridge the gulf between the finite and the infinite. The personality of God is seen through His manifestation of the *Sefirot*.

The *Sefirot* are part of every created thing. Just as the *Sefirot* are contained within God, so they are contained in every being *outside* of God.

The *Sefirot* were created before the physical world. They exist in a world that is above time; in that world, past, present, and future combine. The Yod Hey Vav Hey letters are so powerful that when we focus on them, or if we speak them, they have a direct relationship with this physical world. Indeed, the Jewish mystics believe that these letters were present at Creation and that God used the instruments of these letters in His Creation. The interaction of these letters within the *Sefirot* took place even before the creation of our physical universe according to the Jewish mystics.

5. Moses Cordovero (1522–1570) was the foremost Kabbalist of his era, according to Yitzchak Luria (the Ari). Cordovero's first major work, *Pardes Rimonim,* is an encyclopedic work documenting Cordovero's Kabbalistic system. He lived in Safed, studied under Rabbi Joseph Caro (author of the *Shulkhan Aruch*), and established a seminary for Kabbalah. Among his students was Chaim Vital.

6. Mystic Judaism believes that a divine light shines in all things. And the goal of the person who does meditative prayer or meditations is to penetrate the shell of existence and to establish contact with this inner light, which is the dimension of divinity.

7. This table is based on Moses Cordovero, *Pardes Rimonim,* Sha'ar Shem ben Dalet, Gate 19, Chapter 4.

SOURCES

Chapter 1: God is a Force in the Universe and in Us

6   . . . : Ibn al-Arabi of Islam . . .: Muhyiddin Ibn' Arabi, *Journey to the Lord of Power: A Sufi Manual on Retreat*. Translated by Rabia Terri Harris (New York: Inner Traditions International, Ltd., 1981).

7   Rabbi Joseph Albo . . . identifies light and God . . .: Joseph Rabbi Albo, *Sefer Ikkarim* (Vilna, Rabbi Ponek, 1882), part 2, chapter 29, pp. 95–96.

7–8 The Jewish Kabbalist Joseph Ergas . . .: Joseph Ergas, *Shomer Emunim* (Jerusalem, 1925), chapter 2, p. 11.

12   Daniel Stern shows that . . .: Daniel Stern, *The Interpersonal World of the Human Infant* (New York: Basic Books, 1985), pp. 41–42.

13   Strange is our . . .: Albert Einstein, "The Meeting Place of Science and Religion." In *Has Science Discovered God?*, Edward Cotton, ed. (Freeport, New York: Books for Libraries Press, 1931), p. 93.

Chapter 3: The Greater Mind

24   Everyone who serves God . . .: Levi Yitzchak, *Kedushat Levi* (Slavuta, Ukraine, 1798; reprint: Brooklyn: Rabbi Fishmann, 1977) p. 46.

25   This is why the commentators . . .: Levi Yitzchak, *ibid.*

28   because he did the will of Him at whose word . . .: William G. Braude and Israel J. Kapstein, trans., *Tanna Debe Eliyyahu: The Lore of the School of Elijah* (Philadelphia: Jewish Publication Society of America, 5741/1981), p. 91.

34   One must believe . . .: Rabbi Aaron of Apt, ed., *Keter Shem Tov: The Teachings of Rabbi Israel Ba'al Shem Tov* (1794; reprint: Brooklyn: Kehot Publication Society, 1987), section 80.

36   False humility . . .: Rabbi Aaron of Apt, section 145.

39   He who knows . . .: Paul Brunton, *The Notebooks of Paul Brunton:* Vol. 1, *Perspectives* (Burdett, NY: Larson Publications, 1984), p. 275.

40   Just believing a set of facts . . .: Agnes Sanford, *The Healing Light* (New York: Ballantine Books, 1947), p. 28.

41   remember to live . . .: Paul Brunton, Vol. 15, *Advanced Contemplation*, p. 90.

41   The student must place this seed-thought . . .: Paul Brunton, Vol. 1, *Perspectives*, p. 155.

Chapter 4: Practicing the Presence of God

450   The greater the person . . .: Ha-Rav Abraham Kook, *Lights of Holiness*, Vol. 3 (Jerusalem: Mosad Ha-Rav Kook, 1945), p. 270.

47   cases of group mysticism.: Thomas R. Kelly, *The Gathered Meeting* (Philadelphia, PA: The Tract Association of Friends), p. 1

48   The healing powers . . .: Paul Brunton, *The Notebooks of Paul Brunton:* Vol. 7, *Healing of the Self* (Burdett, NY: Larson Publications, 1987), p. 26.

49   It is possible . . . : Paul Brunton, Vol. 7, *Healing of the Self,* p. 29.

49   Brunton offers a healing practice . . .: See Paul Brunton, Vol. 7, *Healing of the Self,* pp. 30–34.

49   There are no miracles . . . : Paul Brunton, *The Notebooks of Paul Brunton:* Vol. 1, *Perspectives* (Burdett, NY: Larson Publications, 1984), p. 121.

Chapter 5: Healing Prayer

53   Rabbi Chiya bar Abba was ill. . . .: *Talmud Bavli:* Tractate *Berachos,* Artscroll Series/Schottenstein Edition (Brooklyn: Nesorah Publications, 1997), volume I, p. 5b.

56 And come and see . . . . : Rabbi Simeon bar Yochai (Moses de Leon), *Sefer Ha-Zohar*, with Sulam Commentary, translated by Rabbi Yehuda Lev Ashlag (Jerusalem, no date), p. 57a.

Chapter 6: The Commandment to Rejoice

64 As we thank Thee . . .: Central Conference of American Rabbis, ed., *Union Prayer Book*. (New York: Central Conference of American Rabbis, 1962), part II, p. 8.

66 News was brought . . . : Martin Buber, *Tales of the Hasidim: Later Masters* (New York: Schocken Books, 1948), p. 90.

68 They who keep the Sabbath . . . : *Union Prayer Book*, op. cit., part I, p. 32.

68 The Jewish mystic Chaim Vital wrote in the introduction. . .: Chaim Vital, *Sha'ar Ha-Kavvanot* (Jerusalem: Yeshivat Kol Yehuda, 1945), part 1, p. 2.

69 According to Martin Buber, Rabbi Nachman . . . : Martin Buber, *Tales of Rabbi Nachman*, (New York: Horizon Press, 1956), p. 3.

69 . . . *mitzvah gedolah* . . .: Rabbi Nachman of Bratslav, *Likutey Moharan: The Collected Teachings of Rabbi Nachman of Bratslav* (Jerusalem, 1928), vol. 2, paragraph 24, p. 22b.

69 It is a great *mitzvah* . . .: Rabbi Nachman of Bratslav, *ibid.*

71 Several Hasidim . . .: Lewis I. Newman, *The Hasidic Anthology* (New York: Charles Scribner Sons, 1934), p. 88.

71-2 The capacity to enjoy . . . : Heinz Kohut, in Elson, Miriam, ed., *The Kohut Seminars*, on Self Psychology and Psychotherapy with Adolescents and Young Adults (New York: W.W. Norton & Company, 1987), pp. 308–309.

72 . . . a review of research on depression.: Hara Estroff Marano, "Depression: Beyond Serotonin," in *Psychology Today*, 32, no. 2 (March/ April 1999), pp. 32–33.

72 . . . we require a self that has cohesion, strength, and harmony.: Heinz Kohut, *How Does Analysis Cure?* (Chicago: University of Chicago Press, 1984), p. 52.

72   We need to feel alive, real and worthwhile: Heinz Kohut, in
     Elson, Miriam, ed., *The Kohut Seminars*, p. 53.

72   empathic resonance . . .sustained . . .: Heinz Kohut, *How Does
     Analysis Cure?*, p. 70.

74   Rabbi Nachman said, "Through depressions . . .: In Perle
     Besserman, ed., *The Way of the Jewish Mystics* (Boston: Shambhala
     Publications, 1994), pp. 179–180.

75   The Ba'al Shem Tov wrote, "When a person is happy . . .: In
     Pearle Besserman, ed., p. 181.

Chapter 7: Let Us Make Man in Our Image

82   All the time the body . . .: Shabbetai Donnolo, *Sefer Hachmonin*
     in *Sefer Yetzirah* (Jerusalem: Yeshivat Kol Yehuda, 1990), p. 126.

83   The body is a garment . . .: Chaim Vital, *Sha'arei Kedushah:
     Gates of Holiness* (Jerusalem: Eshkol Publishing), chapter 1: Gate
     1, p. 6.

85   Let us make man . . .: Joseph Caro, *Sefer Maggid Meshirim*, trans-
     lated from Aramaic to Hebrew by Yechiel Avraham Bar Lev
     (Jerusalem: Brumstein Publishing, 1990), pp. 24–25.

91   I have always desired . . .: Saint Térèsa of Lisieux, "The Little
     Way" in *Teachings of the Christian Mystics*, Andrew Harvey, ed.
     and trans. (Boston: Shambhala, 1998), pp. 168–169.

92   splendid in mind and heart also.: Shinichi Suzuki, *Nurtured by
     Love, A New Approach to Education* (Smithtown, New York:
     Exposition Press, 1969), pp. 26–27.

92   To make a resolution . . .; Through repeated practice . . .; To
     foster intuition . . .; habit of action . . . is the most important
     thing . . .: Shinichi Suzuki, p. 56; p. 57; p. 63; p. 100.

Chapter 8: Alternative Meditations

99   For when the world was created . . .: Rabbi Simeon bar Yochai,
     Zohar, translated by Harry Sperling and Maurice Simon (London:
     Soncino Press, 1970), vol. 2, p. 111.

100 There are 22 foundation letters. . . .: *Sefer Yetzirah*, chapter 2, Mishnah 2, p. 38.

102 Moses Cordovero in his text . . .: Moses Cordevero, *Pardes Rimonim* (Karetz, 1786) Gate 21: Sha'ar Shem ben Dalet, chapter 4, p. 84.

106 . . . which is like that of the Sapphire.: Gershom Scholem, *Kabbalah* (New York: Dutton Signet, 1990), pp. 99–100.

106 The *Sefirot* both individually and collectively . . .: Gershom Scholem, p. 105.

106 . . . identical with God's Essence.: Gershom Scholem, p. 101.

106 . . . the first three *Sefirot* represent the evolution from Will to Thought.: Gershom Scholem, pp. 109–110.

108 He teaches in his book . . .: Moses Cordovero, *Pardes Rimonim*, Sha'ar Shem ben Dalet, Gate 19, Chapter 4, p. 84.

110 It is good and pleasant . . .: Moses Cordovero, *Pardes Rimonim*, chapter 32: Gate *Sha'ar Ha-Kavvanah*, p. 168.

111 In many places in Kabbalistic texts . . . colors . . .: Moses Cordovero, *Pardes Rimonim*, Gate 10, Chapter 1, p. 48.

111 Colors that are seen . . .: Moses Cordovero, *ibid.*

112 Thus if one wishes to bring down . . .: Moses Cordovero, *ibid.*

114 there are millions and millions . . .: Gary Zukav, *The Dancing Wu-Li Masters: An Overview of the New Physics* (New York: William Morrow, 1979), p. 58.

114 although Newton's physics . . .: Gary Zukav, p. 46.

115 The most beautiful thing . . . devoutly religous men.: Einstein, Albert. "The Meeting Place of Science and Religion," in *Has Science Discovered God? A Symposium of Modern Scientific Opinion* (Freeport, NY: Books for Libraries Press. 1931), pp. 96–97.

119 Do His will as though . . . : Philip Blackman, ed., *Ethics of the Fathers* (New York: Judaica Press, 1990), chapter 2, mishna 4, vol. 4. p. 498.

Chapter 9: Our Prayer Group

123   . . . traditional *Mi Shebeirach* prayer . . . O God who blessed our
        ancestors . . .: In Rabbi David Polish, ed., Reform Rabbi's Manual
        (New York: Central Conference of American Rabbis, 1988), p.
        196.

125   Rabbi Eliezer began a commentary . . .: Yochai, Rabbi Simeon
        bar (Moses de Leon), *Sefer Ha-Zohar*, with Sulam Commentary,
        translated by Rabbi Yehuda Lev Ashlag. (Jerusalem, no date),
        Parashat Naso, volume 7, p. 31.

126   But when the *Shekhina* precedes . . .: Rabbi Simeon bar Yochai,
        Parashat Naso, ibid.

132   experience of the availability . . .: Heinz Kohut, *How Does Analysis
        Cure?* (Chicago: University of Chicago Press, 1984), p. 70.

133   In our endeavour to understand . . .: Albert Einstein and Infeld,
        Leopold, *The Evolution of Physics* (New York: Simon and Schuster,
        1938), p. 31.

136   . . . laws relative to the *Amidah,* in the *Shulkhan Aruch,* Section
        Orach Chayyim: Joseph Caro, *Shulkhan Aruch* ([*Sefer Megene Eretz*]
        Israel, 1969), volume I, p. 76.

BIBLIOGRAPHY

"A.D.D. WareHouse." 300 Northwest 70th Avenue, Suite 102, Plantation, FL 33317. 800-792-8944.

Albo, Joseph Rabbi. *Sefer Ikkarim* (Vilna Edition), Part 2. Vilna: Rabbi Ponek, 1882.

Apt, Rabbi Aaron of, ed. *Keter Shem Tov: The Teachings of Rabbi Israel Ba'al Shem Tov.* (1794) Brooklyn: Kehot Publication Society, 1987.

Barakat, Abdul. *Kitab al-Mu'tabar* (Arabic text). Edited by Serefettin Altkaya. Hyderabad, 1939. 3 volumes.

Barkley, Russell A. *Taking Charge of ADHD: The Complete Authoritative Guide for Parents.* New York: The Guilford Press, 1995.

Besserman, Perle, ed. *The Way of the Jewish Mystics.* Boston: Shambhala Publications, 1994.

Blackman, Philip, ed. *Ethics of the Fathers.* New York: Judaica Press, 1990.

Braude, William G. and Israel J. Kapstein, trans. *Tanna Debe Eliyyahu: The Lore of the School of Elijah.* Philadelphia: Jewish Publication Society of America, 5741/1981.

Brunton, Paul. *The Notebooks of Paul Brunton:* Vol. 1, *Perspectives.* Burdett, NY: Larson Publications, 1984.

———. *The Notebooks of Paul Brunton:* Vol. 7, *Healing of the Self.* Burdett, NY: Larson Publications, 1987.

———. *The Notebooks of Paul Brunton:* Vol. 15, *Advanced Contemplation.* Burdett, NY: Larson Publications, 1988.

Buber, Martin. *Tales of the Hasidim: Later Masters.* New York: Schocken Books, 1948.

———. *Tales of Rabbi Nachman.* New York: Horizon Press, 1956.

Caro, Joseph. *Sefer Maggid Meshirim.* Translated from Aramaic to Hebrew by Yechiel Avraham Bar Lev. Jerusalem: Brumstein Publishing, 1990.

———. *Shulkhan Aruch.* (*Sefer Megene Eretz*) Israel, 1969.

Central Conference of American Rabbis, ed. *Union Prayer Book.* New York: Central Conference of American Rabbis, 1962.

Chan, Luke. "A Visit to An Unique Qigong Hospital," in *T'ai Chi: The International Magazine of T'ai Chi Ch'uan* 19, no. 5 (October 1995): 34–35.

Cordovero, Moses. *Pardes Rimonim.* Karetz, 1786.

Donnolo, Shabbetai. *Sefer Hachmonin* in *Sefer Yetzirah.* Jerusalem: Yeshivat Kol Yehuda, 1990.

Dowling, Colette. *You Mean I Don't Have to Feel This Way?* New Help for Depression, Anxiety, and Addiction. New York: Charles Scribner's Sons, 1991.

Dostoyevsky, Fyodor. *The Brothers Karamazov.* New York: Penguin Books, 1958.

Einstein, Albert. "The Meeting Place of Science and Religion." In *Has Science Discovered God?,* Edward Cotton, ed. Freeport, NY: Books for Libraries Press, 1931.

——— and Infeld, Leopold. *The Evolution of Physics.* New York: Simon and Schuster, 1938.

Elson, Miriam, ed. *The Kohut Seminars,* on Self Psychology and Psychotherapy with Adolescents and Young Adults. New York: W.W. Norton & Company, 1987.

Ergas, Joseph. *Shomer Emunim.* Jerusalem, 1925.

Ginzberg, Louis. *Legends of the Jews.* Philadelphia: Jewish Publication Society of America, 1968.

Goldin, Hyman, trans. *Pirke Avot* (*Ethics of the Fathers*). New York: Hebrew Publishing Company, 1962.

Green, Rabbi Arthur, "Teachings of the Hasidic Masters." In *Back to the Sources*, Barry Holtz, ed. Philadelphia: The Jewish Publication Society of America, 1984.

Hallowell, Edward M., M.D. and John J. Ratey, M.D. *Driven to Distraction: Recognizing and Coping with Attention Deficit Disorder from Childhood through Adulthood.* New York: Simon & Schuster, 1994.

Harvey, Andrew. *Teachings of the Christian Mystics.* Boston: Shambhala Publications, 1998.

Holtz, Barry, ed. *Back to the Sources.* Philadelphia: The Jewish Publication Society of America, 1984.

The Holy Bible. New Revised Standard Version. Oxford, England: Oxford University Press, 1989.

The Holy Scriptures. Philadelphia: Jewish Publication Society of America, 1982.

Ibn' Arabi, Muhyiddin. *Journey to the Lord of Power: A Sufi Manual on Retreat.* Translated by Rabia Terri Harris. New York: Inner Traditions International, Ltd., 1981.

Kahn, Michael. *Between Therapist and Client: The New Relationship.* New York: W.H. Freeman and Co., 1991.

Kaplan, Aryeh. *Jewish Meditation.* New York: Schocken Books, Inc., 1985.

Keating, Thomas. *Open Mind, Open Heart: The Contemplative Dimensions of the Gospel.* New York: Continuum Publishing Company, 1995.

Kelly, Thomas. *The Gathered Meeting.* Philadelphia: The Tract Association of Friends.

Kohut, Heinz, M.D.. *How Does Analysis Cure?* Chicago: University of Chicago Press, 1984.

———. *The Kohut Seminars,* on Self Psychology with Adolescents and Young Adults. Miriam Elson, ed. New York: W.W. Norton & Company, 1987.

Kook, Ha-Rav Abraham. *Lights of Holiness,* Vol. 3. Jerusalem: Mosad Ha-Rav Kook, 1945.

Marano, Hara Estroff,. "Depession: Beyond Serotonin," in *Psychology Today,* 32, no. 2 (March/April 1999), pp. 32–33.

Marone, Nicky. *Women and Risk: How to Master Your Fears and Do What You Never Thought You Could Do.* New York: St. Martin's Press, 1992.

Marvege, Jacob. *She'elot u–Teshuvot min ha-Shamayyim* (*Responsa from Heaven*). Tel Aviv: Gitler Publishing, 1939.

Mitchell, Hobart. *Prayer for Healing.* Worcester, MA: Mosher Book and Tract Committee, New England Yearly Meeting of Friends, 901 Pleasant St., Worcester, MA 06012, 1991.

Nachman, Rabbi of Bratslav. *Likutey Moharan: The Collected Teachings of Rabbi Nachman of Bratslav.* Jerusalem, 1928.

The New American Bible: The New Catholic Translation. New York: Thomas Nelson, Publishers, 1971.

Newman, Lewis I. *The Hasidic Anthology.* New York: Charles Scribner Sons, 1934.

Polish, Rabbi David, ed. *Reform Rabbi's Manual.* New York: Central Conference of American Rabbis, 1988.

Rand, William. *Reiki, The Healing Touch, First and Second Degree Manual.* Southfield, MI: Vision Publications, 1991.

Robbins, Anthony. *Awaken the Giant Within: How to take immediate control of your mental, emotional, physical & financial destiny.* New York: Simon and Schuster, 1991.

Rogers, Carl. *On Becoming a Person.* Boston: Houghton Mifflin Co., 1961.

Sanford, Agnes. *The Healing Light.* New York: Ballantine Books, 1947.

Scholem, Gershom. *Kabbalah.* New York: Dutton Signet, 1990.

Schwartz, Jeffrey M. *Brain Lock: Free Yourself from Obsessive-Compulsive Behavior.* New York: HarperCollins, 1996.

Sefer Yetzirah. Jerusalem: Yeshivat Kol Yehuda, 1990.

Stengel, Melinda. "Parents Can Help Girls Win Confidence Game," in *The Chicago Tribune,* May 11, 1997, Section 13.

Stern, Daniel. *The Interpersonal World of the Human Infant.* New York: Basic Books, 1985.

Suzuki, Shinichi. *Nurtured by Love: A New Approach to Education.* Smithtown, NY: Exposition Press, 1969.

Talmud Bavli: Tractate *Berachos* (Artscroll Series/Schottenstein Edition), Volume I. Brooklyn: Nesorah Publications, 1997.

Vital, Chaim. *Etz Ha-Hayyim.* No date.

———. *Sha'ar Ha-Kavvanot.* Jerusalem: Yeshivat Kol Yehuda, 1945.

———. *Sha'arei Kedushah: Gates of Holiness.* Jerusalem, Eshkol Publishing, no date.

Wade, Chris, ed. The Center for Reiki Training Web Site Page. 1996.

Waldholz, Michael. "Panic Pathway: Study of Fear Shows Emotions Can Alter 'Wiring' of the Brain." In *The Wall Street Journal,* September 29, 1993.

Yitzchak, Levi. *Kedushat Levi.* (Slavuta, Ukraine, 1798) Brooklyn: Rabbi Fishmann, 1977.

Yochai, Rabbi Simeon bar (Moses de Leon). *Sefer Ha-Zohar,* with Sulam Commentary. Translated by Rabbi Yehuda Lev Ashlag. Jerusalem, no date.

———. *Zohar.* Translated by Harry Sperling and Maurice Simon. London: Soncino Press, 1970.

Zukav, Gary, *The Dancing Wi-Li Masters: An Overview of the New Physics.* New York: William Morrow, 1979.

INDEX